T0299694

Print Production

A Complete Guide to Planning, Printing and Packaging

Published in Great Britain by
Laurence King
An imprint of Quercus Editions Ltd
Carmelite House
50 Victoria Embankment
London EC4Y 0DZ
An Hachette UK company

LE GUIDE DE LA FABRICATION
© EDITIONS PYRAMYD, 2021
English translation © Laurence King 2023

A CIP catalogue record for this book is available from the British Library
HB ISBN 978-1-52943-016-5
EBOOK ISBN 978-1-52943-015-8

10 9 8 7 6 5 4 3 2 1

Originally published in French as *Le guide de la fabrication: Comprendre, gérer et imprimer vos productions graphiques*
This edition published by arrangement with Pyramyd, Paris
English translation by Andrea Reece

French edition team:
Editorial director: Céline Remechido
Project editor: Christelle Doyelle
Graphic design: Caroline Moutier

English edition team:
Project editor: Liz Faber
Layout designer: Ginny Zeal
Production manager: Claire Keep

Printed and bound in China by C&C Offset Printing Co., Ltd.

Margherita Mariano

Print Production

A Complete Guide to Planning, Printing and Packaging

Laurence King

CONTENTS

INTRODUCTION

A MATTER OF TRUST

You are asked to produce a printed object of some kind – an invitation card, poster, brochure, magazine, annual report, catalogue or book. Whatever the object, the issues are the same: you either know a lot, a little, or nothing at all about the technical side. Production isn't your profession. Even though you're interested in it, you're apprehensive about this stage because of its multiple challenges: a budget to manage, a deadline to meet, and a certain level of quality to ensure. You might feel the same kind of trepidation when you take your car to the garage or go to the dentist or entrust any kind of expert with a critical job without having total control over what they do, and without knowing whether the final bill with which you are presented is entirely justified.

The best solution is to choose your specialists well and trust them.

This book aims to give you the fundamental information you need to be able to ask yourself and others the right questions at the right time, without necessarily mastering the myriad technical details that constantly evolve as the technology advances.

Producing printed material, just like making clothes or building a house, requires a range of different skills in different professions. As you cannot acquire these skills overnight (a lifetime is not long enough), focus on what you can do and identify the key issues. You've bought a house off-plan, now it's down to the different trades to lay the bricks, install the plumbing, fit the windows and lay the tiles you've chosen, achieving the right balance between your personal taste and expert advice. The professionals you work with will bring your ideas to life, and there's no reason why this won't lead to a successful outcome. Your task consists of choosing the professionals well and letting them get on with their job so they trust you too.

There has to be mutual trust for everything to work.

If you make the error of inputting the wrong product reference on an online sales site, you might lose business or customers but your mistake will have zero material cost because, at this point, it's all just online. However, if you mismanage the production of an annual report, a book or a magazine, thousands or tens of thousands of dollars' worth of printed paper could be wasted.

Therefore, the initial questions you need to ask are not about paper texture, colour management or print format. No, the real question is: who makes the decisions? Who is in charge, whose money is it and who is responsible to whom?

So the first questions that need to be answered before discussing the technical side are: **who makes the decisions and who pays?**

If it's you, you are going to make a commitment to one or several professionals, who will in turn take on suppliers and subcontractors based on your instructions. Depending on your needs, formulate your requests and pay attention to everything that a professional – repro expert, paper producer, printer, screen printer – recommends or advises against. Choose people who are specialists in their field and listen to them. Once you are happy with the options you're being offered, you can sign the relevant quote with peace of mind and start the job.

However, if it's not you who has the final say and signs the cheques, you must put in place a system for the required authorization process before each decisive step (we will explore these steps in subsequent chapters).

The history of print production is littered with regrettable episodes where those in charge of communication enthusiastically went along with the recommendations made by their graphic designer without having fully understood them, and hastily authorized choices of paper, illustrations and image processing. Then, at the last minute, these choices were rejected by a senior manager who was looking at the file for the first time and decided not to approve all or part of the project because they had imagined something different. This can completely derail a production process with logistically or financially irretrievable consequences.

In order to avoid these unfortunate misunderstandings, be specific, factual, repeat everything and follow procedures to the letter. Before committing to a budget, **get the project authorized on a step-by-step basis**, providing samples, tests, mock-ups and anything else that can give a clear idea to those who are paying without actually running the operation. Make sure all communication and authorization is in writing, and use email in preference to texts, which are not only invasive but also unreliable when it comes to traceability.

Managing a project well means taking the time before and during the process to avoid wasting time and money when the printing goes wrong and you have to go back to square one.

Successful printing means having great material that will help boost the sales or circulation of a product, a book, or an idea.
The keywords are: **common sense, rigour** and **foresight**.
The four key tasks are: **define responsibilities, plan, check, monitor**.

To put you on the right track, you'll find a **CHECKLIST** at the end of each chapter summarizing the key steps so you can quickly take stock as you go.

There is an **INDEX** at the back of the book with the terminology for each production phase so you have the vocabulary necessary to discuss issues with your service providers.

We will often be asking **AWKWARD QUESTIONS** to show that there is no such thing as a bad question when it comes to production – and I strongly encourage you not to be shy when it comes to asking any question at all. As all anthropologists know, doubt is a natural function related to the survival instinct; clearing up doubt is the best way to gain knowledge and move forward with confidence because it is safe to do so.

And, as there's nothing like experience to make things stick in the mind, you'll find some **TIPS**, and examples of traps I've fallen into, which I call **BANANA SKINS**. Nobody's perfect!

I

GET ORGANIZED

There's no point in lying: production is not a relaxing activity, especially for those who suddenly find themselves having to produce printed materials with no manufacturing experience. A production manager needs a buyer's ruthlessness, a psychologist's listening skills, the organizational ability of a kids' camp counsellor, the gift of ubiquity, and an unswerving capacity to fix failures, delays and other human weaknesses whenever they arise, which means always foreseeing the unforeseeable.

However, it doesn't require superpowers; it just boils down to **concentration and common sense**. Anyone can manage the production of a printed object if they are inquisitive and organized. To see your project through successfully, you just need to be smart enough to use the expertise of the service providers whom you have chosen wisely. Production is a short or long chain of different trades that must be perfectly aligned and interlock like links in a real chain: your task is to keep an eye on the chain to spot any weaknesses and make sure operations run smoothly.

The process for producing a book, a magazine, a flyer or a simple invitation card is virtually the same, and **the key to producing it well is foresight**. Therefore, you shouldn't finalize the design of your product – format, paper type, layout and binding – before consulting a printer. If finalizing the design is the first thing on your list, you might:

1 — discover too late that your printer's lead time exceeds your deadline, which will jeopardize the outcome of your project, even if you do manage to achieve the quality you want;

2 — end up paying much more than you need to because the production tool might have to be adapted to your specifications and that's not necessarily good on the financing side (a good production manager designs the product based on using existing tools to their best advantage);

3 — find yourself faced with a technical difficulty that means you either have to find other suppliers urgently, or pay a huge surcharge to the service provider that you took on too hastily and whose machinery is not suitable for your project.

So we start at the end: **by what date does the product need to be made?** That is the first issue that needs addressing.

The second concerns **the nature and scope of the product**, so you can establish a framework in terms of price and quality.

The third is to draw up **a description, a schedule and a budget**, so you can ensure these three intrinsic elements are properly coordinated, thus enabling you to stay on track with the help of all those involved.

The brief

When you are producing a printed object, you start with the page layout and image processing, then you send the files to a printer. But production begins well before that and – we can't emphasize this enough – with intelligent planning and keeping the end product in mind.

Don't be surprised if the first questions that need to be asked are not about the first phases of actual production. You have a more or less defined idea of the product you want to make. **Start by describing it in as much detail as possible** and you will see straight away what is clear and what needs to be examined in greater depth.

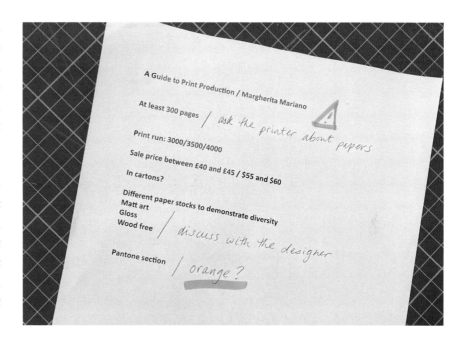

There are various ways to proceed

– You have an in-house production service, in which case, what are you waiting for?
– You don't have one, so these are your options:
  – reach out to a freelance production manager or a production print services company who will operate as your production department.
  – ask around your network for recommendations for a good printer. Some share their knowledge and provide a consultancy service worth its weight in gold, even if their prices are sometimes higher. Bear in mind that a bodged production can cost even more.
– Read this guide! If you open this book in search of salvation only when you find yourself deep in trouble, you might just find the solution to your problem. But if you're a complete beginner (or almost), it's best to leaf through it before you find yourself in a difficult situation.

You're unfamiliar with the technical terminology

If that's your only problem, you're home and dry! Producers, repro specialists and printers all have a built-in translator in their heads that understands what you want, your questions and your shortcomings. That said, their brains aren't connected to yours via Bluetooth, so you need to **avoid making assumptions**. 'That goes without saying', 'that's obvious', 'we always do it like that, don't we?' are expressions that have been heard a thousand times by professionals struggling to decipher a problem caused by a simple instruction that has been misunderstood and that is either impossible, costly or time-consuming to correct at a late stage.

Foresight is action

The description must be as complete as possible and cover every single detail, including information about packaging and shipping requirements. Imagine you are going to deliver 3,000 exhibition catalogues to an art gallery in the city centre and, on the day in question, the truck ends up in a one-way street with no parking bay nearby and the books loose on a pallet that the delivery driver refuses to unload. All this on a rainy afternoon, one hour before the exhibition opens. Panic stations!

Stage 4: refining the layout and proofreading the text as actual production gets underway.

All you had to do was to explain the delivery requirements to your printer and they would have provided a small van with a tail lift, a pallet jack and five-kilo boxes that the gallery assistants would have been able to carry into the gallery after unloading the pallet onto the pavement. They could then have called in a specialist pallet removal company. Efficient. No mess. We'll see as we go through the different phases of production that **paying attention to every single detail in advance** will save you time and money. It will also do wonders for your reputation with your boss or customer by sparing them any extra hassle.

2

The Schedule

The production chain for printed material is a relay race that involves passing the baton; it requires coordination and precision because some operations overlap and some roles are interchangeable.

1 — Collate the text and the digital or analogue images (transparencies, slides, opaque documents such as photographic prints or physical artworks);

2 — analyze image quality and resolution before moving on to layout and again after layout using in-built preflights in InDesign;

3 — put together a mock-up;

4 — fine-tune the layout and proofread the text;

5 — process the images to optimize the colour rendering, do the proofs and make corrections if necessary;

6 — create the PDF files and send them to the printer;

7 — approve the plotter from the printer's Raster Image Processor (RIP)

8 — print;

9 — approve the printed sheets before finishing, if appropriate to schedule and project requirements;

10 - finishing;

11 – confirm the packaging and shipping instructions;

12 - approve the sample copies;

13 - give the green light for delivery;

14 - check and approve the invoice before payment.

The different stages of the production schedule for the French edition of this book	2019								
	JUNE	JULY	AUGUST	SEPTEMBER	OCTOBER	NOVEMBER	DECEMBER	JANUARY	
RELEASE IN BOOKSTORES									
DELIVERY TO WAREHOUSE									
PRINTING									
PAPER ORDER									
MOCK-UP									
REPRO									
PROOFREADING									
FINALIZING IMAGE SEARCHES									
EDITING									
INITIAL IMAGE SEARCHES							▓	▓	▓
WRITING				▓	▓	▓	▓	▓	▓
FIRST FLATPLAN			▓	▓					
DEFINING THE SUBJECT/ SIGNING THE CONTRACT	▓	▓							

										2021	
\	\	\	\	\	\	\	\	\	\	\	\
APRIL	MAY	JUNE	JULY	AUGUST	SEPTEMBER	OCTOBER	NOVEMBER	DECEMBER	JANUARY	FEBRUARY	MARCH
											■
										■	
									■		
							■				
		▓	▓	▓	▓	▓	▓	▓			
								▓			
								▓			
					▓	▓	▓				
		▓	▓	▓	▓	▓	▓				
▓	▓										
▓	▓	▓									

2020

Good planning is the basis for success, much more so than your specific skills. However, it's not simply about following this chronology from one day to the next but about organizing yourself according to what will happen later by anticipating the successive stages. You don't choose the paper the day before sending the files to the printer, but well before this time: weeks or even months in advance, depending on the nature of the product and the type of paper. If your customer or graphic designer has chosen a speciality paper requiring a long manufacturing process that is incompatible with the deadline, you'll have time to change it by consulting your printer well in advance; they will be able to offer you alternatives if necessary.

A paper order largely depends on paper type and the nature of your product: paper for business cards or flyers can be available almost immediately; an invitation printed on speciality paper may take a few days; more complex products may take one to six weeks (see pages 32 and 123).

IF IT'S URGENT IT ALWAYS COSTS MORE

Requesting an urgent delivery with a very short deadline often entails using equipment and staff or subcontractors outside the usual sphere of your service provider; this can have significant cost implications. However, you may be able to get good deals if you commission work with flexible deadlines during your provider's slack periods. Repro studios and printers often specialize in a particular area and, consequently, their order books are full in certain periods or seasons (school textbooks, coffee table books for the Christmas season, monthly or weekly publications). They will be happy to have their presses running outside peak production periods and may be more willing to offer you discounts if they can slot your order into a gap in their schedule.

What to do, by when?

If you can, **communicate to your service provider the known and non-negotiable dates on your calendar** when you request a price. This will provide your printer with clarity and they will be able to plan for and cost the operations to be carried out as accurately as possible, based on your dates.

If you haven't already set the dates, ask your printer to tell you what their requirements are when they send the quote: you will then know what to expect for a possible paper order, which could then determine your other deadlines.

Bear in mind that a printer is dealing with complex logistics. If they subcontract all or part of the finishing and binding work, if they need to work with another printing company to apply a varnish, a hot stamp, or silk-screen printing on an invitation card, packaging or cover, they will need to enter these jobs on their calendar along with the time needed to send the materials they have printed to the subcontractor.

THE AWKWARD QUESTION

Why can't I sign off my brief before choosing a printer and agreeing the project with them?

Any aesthetic choice has technical repercussions. You need to print a brochure using a four-colour process and you suddenly realize that your client's logo requires a spot colour (Pantone). You have already placed an order with a printer who has a four-colour press and who will now have to feed the sheets through a second time, doubling the operational costs of setting up their press. It is better to be clear from the outset and consult one or more service providers before placing an order.

3

The budget

Before launching into producing a printed object, you need to have a clear idea of the following elements and the budget implications item by item.

Text: writing, proofreading, copyright.
Illustrations: remuneration for the computer graphics artists, illustrators and photographers; reproduction rights for stock photos.
Layout: graphic design and style guide, execution and layout, inputting corrections.
You then have three main items to cost:
– repro/prepress
– printing/paper/finishing
– packaging/shipping.

It is easy to manage a budget: **just make sure you haven't forgotten anything before requesting a quote, and tick all the boxes** by regularly checking, point by point, that you are on target as the work progresses.

BOOK: Atlas Mondial du tatouage (The World Atlas of Tattoos)
ISBN: 9782350173658

Exchange rate $1 = €0.94
on 16/01/2017

	EDITION 1		REPRINT 1		REPRINT 2		REPRINT 3	
Place printed	China		China		China		Europe	
No. of copies	4000		2621		1535		2000	

PRINTING COSTS

Currency	In dollars	In euros	In dollars	In euros	In dollars	In euros	In dollars	In euros
Printing unit cost	$5.95	€5.85	$6.50	€6.11	$6.22	€5.85	$7.87	€7.40
Printing total cost	$23,800.00	€20,944.00	$17,036.50	€16,014.31	$9,552	€8,979.75	$5,106	€4,800.00

PUBLISHING COSTS

	EDITION 1	REPRINT 1	REPRINT 2	REPRINT 3
Translation	€5,567.00	- €	- €	- €
Colour work	€84.00	- €	- €	- €
Cover design	€300.00	- €	- €	- €
Proofreading	€1,196.00	- €	- €	- €
Total cost	€7,147.00	- €	- €	- €

	EDITION 1	REPRINT 1	REPRINT 2	REPRINT 3
SHIPPING AND CUSTOMS CLEARANCE COSTS	€1,900.00	€1,456.89	€1,071.57	Included in printing

	EDITION 1	REPRINT 1	REPRINT 2	REPRINT 3
TOTAL excl. sales tax	€29,991.00	€17,471.20	€10,051.32	€14,800.00
Unit cost excl. sales tax	€7.50	€6.67	€6.55	€7.40

	EDITION 1	REPRINT 1	REPRINT 2	REPRINT 3
Sales price incl. sales tax	€37.00	€37.00	€37.00	€37.00
Price excl. sales tax	€35.07	€35.07	€35.07	€35.07

These are the different budgets for a book published in France. The first edition was printed in China, as were the second and third editions, but these two reprints no longer include publishing costs. For the fourth edition, printing in Europe means there were no shipping or customs clearance costs for the French publisher.

And what if there are changes to your project?

If you don't have a scalable budget or sales price, remember that every extra penny you spend is one less for your profit margin.

As a general rule, **avoid placing any orders before you have fully determined your parameters**: all too often, you allow yourself a little extra here, a little unforeseen expense there and you completely lose sight of your original budget. But **if a change becomes necessary along the way, have it costed** and approved before moving on to the next phase.

In any event, as soon as any slippage appears likely, call your service provider to see if they can suggest a technical or a strategic solution that will allow you to rebalance the budget and get back on track. When drawing up a budget, always allow a contingency for unforeseen variables such as price rises in shipping fuel and paper.

MONITORING YOUR BUDGET IS VITAL

Your service providers will always be able to advise you; if you have a limited budget (or if your aspirations are limitless) don't tell them they're too expensive. Instead, tell them what sort of figure you have to play with and see what you can buy with it. You will see that you could move money from one item to another and still keep your accounts balanced: you could reduce the number of illustrations to have high-quality repro and proofs or, conversely, keep as many images as possible by proofing a small representative sample that allows you to fine-tune the whole printed object as much as possible without going into the nitty-gritty. Sometimes you can alter one or more basic features to emphasize a detail that's particularly important to you: reducing the paper grammage, the number of pages or even the size of the printed item would allow you to reduce the overall budget so you can finance your dream cover with a special finish, for example.

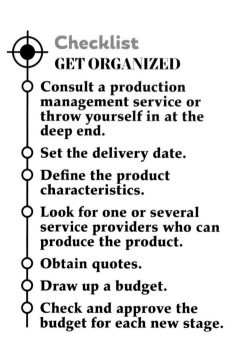

Checklist

GET ORGANIZED

Consult a production management service or throw yourself in at the deep end.

Set the delivery date.

Define the product characteristics.

Look for one or several service providers who can produce the product.

Obtain quotes.

Draw up a budget.

Check and approve the budget for each new stage.

II

FIND THE RIGHT PEOPLE

As you will have realized by now, **producing printed materials requires a team effort.**

Putting together the winning team and defining each person's job is your first task.

You need to find and choose your service providers based on which product or products you are responsible for. You can do this either by consulting the trade press or through recommendation.

The best method is to look at the credits page of a product similar to the one you're planning and see who printed it. You can browse through books and magazines in bookstores, or attend trade fairs and events where there is usually plenty of documentation available.

Word-of-mouth recommendations can also be a great way to find the right people.

Choose a service provider

The criteria for finding the right partner are the same for everyone, but you will need to put them in the order that suits the requirements of your particular project. **Set your priorities!**

Quality

Everyone sees this as a priority, but **quality often comes at a price**. However, paying large sums of money isn't necessarily the key to success. If you're producing a leaflet or a flyer to be distributed free of charge, you don't need to go to a luxury supplier. If you're producing an exhibition catalogue, an annual report, or the prime minister's Christmas cards, you need to make sure your service providers are used to doing this kind of work. It doesn't necessarily have to cost much more if you work with them to define the criteria that allow them to make the best use of their machinery. **Quality also means service**, and service comes from staff availability and good leadership, which has an impact on price. An urgent job often means night work and therefore higher rates. Be aware of what you're aiming for so you know what the next logical step is. A good account controller at your supplier can make all the difference.

Price

It is advisable to compare two or three quotes; logically, you would give the job to the best offer. **It's perfectly normal to negotiate with your service providers. However, avoid treating them as if they were born yesterday** by expecting discounts that are closer to your dreams than the reality of the market – which, of course, they know inside out.

Instead of negotiating on a purely commercial basis, it's in your interest to have an open discussion with the service providers who have given different prices so you can better understand the differences. Don't be afraid to reveal your wish list and put your cards on the table: you may be surprised to find that tweaks and savings are possible without having to ask for a discount. It's not unusual for the printer who starts off being the most expensive to go back to their quote once you've provided extra elements, point out the differences that you may not have noticed between the various quotes, revise their approach and ultimately find they can work within your budget. Curiosity has its rewards! Then you can always ask for a small goodwill gesture: if you've congratulated a printer on their competence, they may be more inclined to want to please you.

Deadlines

If you have time, you can discuss and negotiate to your heart's content. There is a huge and varied range of products on offer, and nowadays it's easy to send files to the other side of the world. But if your deadline is tight, your choice and leeway when it comes to price is reduced in proportion to how long you have. Also, don't imagine that a repro studio, and even less so a printing business, works like a copy shop. Like you, your supplier has certain constraints, and planning work at a production site is not easy, given the number of jobs that are done every day. A printed object may have a global production time of several hours or several days, but the **different production phases do not happen one after the other**. They need to be integrated into an overall, segmented schedule. The delivery dates you are given include the company's internal work-flow management, as well as taking into account possible delays and mishaps, shipping items to subcontractors, etc. If your printer produces a lot of school textbooks, for example, don't give them an urgent job in May the year the Ministry of Education decides to change the curriculum. Knowing a printer's capacity (available machinery) and customer base could help you to choose which one will do the best job at a particular point in time, because everything is relative!

Proximity

If you were hoping to save 20% by printing somewhere cheaper but farther away from you, make sure you have the time to get involved in discussions that could double your production time. If you are in Europe, the UK or the US, printing in Asia requires shipping, which takes about four to six weeks, not to mention customs clearance. If you are in Europe, any business you do within Europe can be slowed down less by physical distance than by language barriers and cultural differences, which (as is the case in other business sectors) set the tone for any business discussions. Either way, make sure your chosen printer has salespeople who speak your language fluently.

One last tip: feel free to choose a printing company a long way away if it suits your requirements, but when it comes to the prepress processing of your images, always go for a supplier in a location you can travel to within a day, or preferably within an hour. It is important to stick to the agreed dates for sending your files to the printer. It's not unusual for things to crop up at the last minute, and it would be a shame if they caused unnecessary difficulties.

Service

Whether the job is going to be done locally or two thousand miles away, **what really makes the difference is the way the job is managed by your contact/account controller at your chosen print supplier**. At your local printer's, you'll probably be dealing directly with the boss, but if you're working with a factory that has dozens or even hundreds of employees, either at home or abroad, make it a priority to build a good working relationship with your account controller. You should expect them to be responsive, to provide complex technical information, to be quick to provide you with quotes and to be available at every stage of the production process. This person will be your guide, your adviser and maybe even your advocate within their company in the event of a problem. **Conflict management is an important part of any business transaction**. You need to be a reliable customer and you need a partner who is equally reliable and open to discussion, including when it comes to thorny issues such as extra costs, quality issues or even late delivery.

Have a look at websites, get information from other customers, and most of all ask for references, samples and mock-ups. You will need them later.

2

The different links in the book production chain

If you don't have a production manager in your team, it is best to define in advance who will take on the role. Many graphic designers have advanced skills in this area and are able to perform the task of monitoring production. Nevertheless, before you start it is vital to make sure they can actually do this and clearly define what they will be doing for the particular project. If you don't do this, **a lack of clarity about who is responsible for what** may creep into your process with regrettable consequences.

Who checks the files before they are sent to the printer? Who draws up the quotes and the purchase orders? Who checks that these elements correspond to what the printer sends you and who signs them off? Who checks the schedule is running smoothly? Who monitors a print run, checks the sheets are correct, gives instructions for packaging, shipping and delivery? Who approves the invoice?

You can cope without a production manager if you don't have the budget for it, but you must be aware of the scale of the task and either take it on yourself with help from your service providers, or assign everyone involved a specific role, without leaving any grey areas.

The terminology in the book production chain was clear twenty years ago, but it is becoming more and more imprecise as technology changes and consequently roles change and overlap.

DTP (computer-assisted page layout/desktop publishing) and the commoditization of the tools involved have generated work segments that can be performed interchangeably by different professionals – in theory at least!

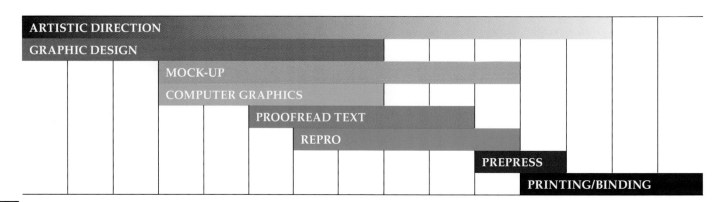

ARTISTIC DIRECTION
GRAPHIC DESIGN
MOCK-UP
COMPUTER GRAPHICS
PROOFREAD TEXT
REPRO
PREPRESS
PRINTING/BINDING

THE AWKWARD QUESTION

Who changes an image, erases a small detail, or adds missing material?

The graphic designer while creating the mock-up? The colour specialist while working on the colour? The DTP operator while making adjustments to the layout file before updating the images? When the person who commissioned the job has not budgeted for these items, which is often the case, everyone hopes that someone else will do them. It is important to define in advance who is being paid for these kinds of tasks, because it's often a source of problems and conflict. If you are selling a graphic design service, ensure the boundaries are clearly defined so you are not asked for more; if you are buying in these services, anticipate what is required and don't profess to think that the other person just has to press a button for something to happen when you can't do it yourself. The smooth running of a production process depends on avoiding conflicts over tasks and corresponding budgets.

Theoretically, anyone can do page layouts or image processing thanks to software such as InDesign, Illustrator or Photoshop. However, that won't make you a graphic designer or a repro expert any more than you can claim to be an architect just because you know how to use AutoCAD. Whether you are an actor or a user in the graphic design field, it might be worth redefining yourself based on the following glossary. You might find that you have bought or sold a service and in fact you were expecting or supplying something different or something extra.

A graphic production project starts with a thought process aimed at establishing a framework for particular content through the choice of typography, materials, formats and overall presentation.

An art director is a designer who comes up with creative solutions and layouts for texts and images and coordinates visual communication to ensure its effectiveness. They are qualified to make choices, give guidelines and supervise the overall monitoring process.

An architect designs a building, then shows how the roof should be made, what floor coverings should be used and how the spaces should be arranged; however, they are not a roofer, tiler or builder, although they have the skills to oversee and guarantee both the solidity of the structure and the design details.

An art director works with one or several **layout designers**. Their work consists of carefully and intelligently flowing the typographic elements and illustrations into a predetermined grid. These days, it's not unusual for a graphic designer to make the initial suggestions and also do the page layout themself.

That's why we have the general term **graphic designer** to describe a professional who can handle typography and page layout as well as image processing, while also having the capacity to make specific propositions in the same way as an art director. They can also take on the role of a **computer graphics designer** – a specialist who creates digital images, colours comics, creates cards, logos and drawings as well as doing creative retouching of images.

What complicates matters is that it is getting harder to distinguish between all these professions. Multi-skilling is a huge asset in the publishing and communications field and is even a necessity, often for purely financial reasons. Increasingly, graphic designers and DTP operators are asked to enter text corrections into the final files, despite the fact that editing or text correcting is not their primary skill.

There can also be different expectations between graphic designers, computer graphics designers and prepress specialists (**colour experts** and **DTP operators**) when it comes to making significant alterations to an image. What is on screen and what will eventually print will be

different, and it's important to communicate what those differences will be and why.

Prepress is the virtual or physical space where everything comes together for a document to be printed correctly.
Every printing company has a prepress department that:
– receives your files and checks them for non-conformities (format or pagination errors, lack of typographical fonts or bleeds, low-resolution images);
– creates an imposition with the elements that will subsequently be placed on the print sheet;
– prepares a control document, known as the plotter, so you can approve the layout of the elements, and creates the plates that will go on the machine after you have given your approval for printing.

Well before that, prepress operations consist of collating the different elements (text, illustrations, graphics, logos). This is done by a graphic designer, who organizes them using page layout software. As we have previously seen, they can also be involved in retouching images, inserting text corrections and creating PDFs for the printer.
Between these two worlds, it is still common (and sometimes strongly recommended) to work with a **repro specialist** whose job is to manage the colours and check that current standards are being applied in the scrupulous preparation of the files to be sent to the **printer.**

Timeline of a production run:
1) the laser output that accompanies the PDF files sent to the printer,
2) the printer's plotter proof that you approve,
3) the sheets to approve before finishing,
4) the sample copy to check before delivery.

3

Communication with your partners

Precisely define the tasks of all parties involved in the processing of images and graphic elements before entering into **an unambiguous contractual relationship** with your two main industrial partners: the repro specialist and the printer.

Steps to follow when you contract a repro service

Ever since DTP software has reduced the time it takes to prepare a pre-press file by a factor of ten, people have tended to treat a repro service like a McDonald's drive-through. However, you need to bear in mind that it is a company like any other, with its own rhythms, deadlines and unalterable workflow.

Plan a schedule and get it approved by the repro expert well before work starts. Giving your repro house clear timeframes and expectations is important. The day you give them the files, clearly indicate the items you have given them, tell them your preferred date for return of any proofs and files you may have requested and the date by which everything has to be finalized. Agree a date for the first colour correction session. Colour correction sessions may involve various people, including authors, editors, graphic designers and your production controller, and you may require the expertise of your repro specialist.

These are the points you need to watch out for when you work with a printer

As production controller, you should build time into the schedule for proofing depending on the type of print job and requirements of your customer or yourself as the client. A full-colour print job will require more time due to the colour proofing process and potential rounds of colour correction. As a rule of thumb, allow at least one month for proofing and a round of correction proofs. For complex colour books such as art or photography titles, if proofs must be matched to actual artworks the proofing process can take considerably longer, especially if the artist or estate has final colour approval.

BANANA SKIN

You can't expect a printer to guess what you have accidentally or negligently forgotten to tell them. Sometimes, they spot what's missing and call you with queries, but unfortunately sometimes they simply follow your omissions to the letter. Incorrect wording relating to size and format could lead to mistakes: if you ask for a '28 × 21 cm [11 × 8 in]' format, it is understood that your book should be printed in a landscape-style format – horizontal, in other words.

The manufacture schedule will mainly be dependent on the type of project you're working on – how long it takes to physically manufacture, especially if there are offline finishing processes and handworking – and the materials you're working with, whether it's local market or stock paper, or 'indented' paper (manufactured for your order), or other special paper or binding material required for the job.

When it comes to larger print runs and specific paper stock, you need to take the longer view.

Printers can work with standard format papers in certain sizes, which they call 'house papers'. These papers, which the printer uses continually in volume and will hold and replenish stocks of, are often convenient to use because the price can be slightly sharper and stocks are easily available for speedy printing. 'Indenting' means the paper stock is produced to the exact size and quantity required for your project so that you achieve the most economical price for your job. However, the trade-off is you have to wait for the paper to be manufactured, which could take anywhere from one to three months depending on paper and printing location, and sometimes longer, for example if you want to use a European paper in the Far East. As a rule of thumb, in Europe indenting paper

lead time is a month or so, and in the Far East it is around two months. The higher the print quantity, the longer your manufacturing schedule will be, especially if you have to factor in indenting the paper. This is a simple fact of manufacturing timescales: it takes longer to make high volumes of paper and longer to process the job through the printing and binding machines. The manufacturing stage will, depending on the printer, usually take anywhere from three weeks (for a speedy reprint), while a more complex project or higher quantity can take five to seven weeks. Printers' schedules also change according to seasonal peaks and troughs of demand, for example in book manufacturing UK printers will be busy from late summer through September in the run-up to Christmas, but likely to be quieter towards New Year and January. Larger publishers will work with their suppliers to balance reprint loadings through the quieter periods to achieve economic pricing, an arrangement that works for both customer and supplier. It's important to factor in that your printer may be closed for public holidays in the country where you are printing, for example Lunar New Year in China.

Being aware of these various timing restrictions and material requirements is essential to plan your projects and work closely with your supplier to ensure you order materials in good time, deliver your files, proofs and various approvals and instructions in order to execute your project in a timely manner.

It's also good practice to allow a little buffer time in your schedules to accommodate unforeseen minor delays that may occur along the way.

This is the correct attitude to take in the event of conflict

When conflict occurs due to poor workmanship or a delay, hubris and dogmatism aren't your best friends. Your service providers are your partners, and a customer has as many obligations as a supplier.

In the event of disputes related to defects or production delays, **manufacturers are often prepared to negotiate**: you must stay firm if your suppliers haven't stuck to what you agreed, but making disproportionate demands or raising your voice will only serve to shut down communication. Be open to dialogue and be conciliatory. As we all know, a good agreement is better than a bad court case (and a service provider usually holds most of the technical cards).

4

Request a quote

On the following page you will find a standard grid for requesting a quote; use it **to check you haven't forgotten anything after you've written your description.**

If you have a complex product and haven't yet decided on all the characteristics, make sure that everyone – including you – can find their way around the grid. Draw up a basic version and then express everything else in the form of **variants** or options, which you may or may not add to your base according to your needs.

If, for example, you have not yet decided on the finishing and binding for your book, you can start with a standard binding and request a **variant** for flexibinding (see page 229). If you've already decided on a standard binding, you might want to come up with a variant for the cover material (laminated paper, cloth or speciality paper).

You can express all non-essentials as **options** A, B or C, which could potentially be added to your basic version depending on your budget and wish list: presentation box, jacket, sticker, ribbon marker.

A book can also be packaged in different ways: individually shrink-wrapped in plastic or several copies placed in cardboard boxes, or both, depending on how fragile your book is and the requirements of your distributor. Many trade printers supply books shrink-wrapped together in multiples. If you do not specify this, you run the risk of receiving your books piled onto a pallet that might be well protected but could still be damaged during transport, in which case you'll have to pay a surcharge to the distributor for repackaging. Ask your printer how they pack their products as standard – they should include this information on their quote, but it is always worth checking.

	DATE
	Updated on:

SCHEDULE

Paper order:

Delivery of files to you:

Delivery to us:

Title:

Print run (+/– × %):   copies and run-on copy

TECHNICAL DESCRIPTION

Closed trimmed Format	Portrait/Landscape	

Number of pages	Number of pages	
	Colours	
	Paper	
Interior 1	Number of pages	
	Colours	
	Paper	
Interior 2	Number of pages	
	Colours	
	Paper	
Finishing	Flat, folded, hardcover, softcover, etc.	

Cover	Colours	
	Paper	
	Laminate	
Options	Dry stamp, hot stamp varnish, screen print…	
	Label, imprint, die cut shape, ribbon marker…	

Endpapers	Colours	
	Paper	
Jacket	Colours	
	Paper	
	Laminate	

Options	…	
Belly band	Height	
	Colours	
	Paper	
	Finish	

Options	…	
Slipcase/ (presentation) box	Colours	
	Paper, card, board	
	Laminate	

Options	…	

Packaging	

Shipping	

Terms of payment	

SCHEDULE

Paper order:	TBC
Delivery of files to you:	15/11/20
Delivery to us:	28/11/20

Title: MAILSHOT LOCAL RESTAURANT

Print run (+/– 5%): 1,000 copies and run-on copy

TECHNICAL DESCRIPTION

Closed trimmed format	15 × 21 cm 6 × 8¼ in (portrait)	(Open 21 × 30 cm/8¼ × 11¾ in)
Number of pages	4	
Colours	4/4*	
Paper	matt coated 170gsm	
Finishing	folded to size…	

Packaging	Shrink-wrapped in bundles of 50 copies

Shipping	Delivery point central Lyon

Terms of payment	By bank transfer within 50 days of delivery

* This could also read 4 colours on both sides

> **※ TIP**
> **Any change to an item is effectively a new quote for an estimator. If there are too many things you are undecided about and too many alternatives, consider several separate requests and call the supplier before putting your request in writing to ensure it is readable and manageable. They will be happy to help you structure your ideas and your order to best effect.**

Sample quote.

SCHEDULE

Paper order:	TBC
Delivery of files:	TBC
Delivery to us:	15/12/2020
	DATE NON-NEGOTIABLE

Title: YIPPEE MAGAZINE

Print run (+/– 3%): 6,000 copies and run-on

TECHNICAL DESCRIPTION

Closed trimmed format	21 × 28.5 cm/ 8¼ × 11¼ in portrait	
Number of pages	128	
Colours	4/4	
Paper	Uncoated white 140gsm	
Finishing	softcover, perfect bound	

Cover	Colours	recto: 4 colours + Pantone, verso: 4 colours
	Paper	Board coated one side 300gsm
	Laminate	Matt

Additional requirements	Spot varnish on 25% of the first page and spine

Packaging	Shrink-wrapped in bundles of 10, on EPAL pallets

Shipping	2 points: 500 copies central Paris (truck with tail lift and pallet jack), the rest to distributor located in departement 76

Terms of payment	30% on order, balance at 60 days

On this page and overleaf: three examples of requests for quotes, from simple to complicated. In the print run section, the +/– followed by a percentage indicates accepted tolerance (see page 131).

DATE 10/10/2020

SCHEDULE	
Paper order:	TBC
Delivery of files to you:	END NOVEMBER 2020
Delivery to us:	MID-JANUARY 2020

Title:	ROYAL HOTEL

Print run(+/– × %):	1,500 copies and run-on

CHANGE OF LANGUAGE BLACK TEXT AND COMPLETE CHANGE OF COVER AND JACKET

COMPRISING	1,000	FRENCH
	500	ENGLISH

TECHNICAL DESCRIPTION

Closed trimmed format	28 × 22 cm/11 × 8½ in landscape	
Number of pages		
Interior 1	Number of pages	112 (7 signatures of 16 pages)
	Colours	4/4 + Pantone silver
	Paper	Coated matt 150gsm
Interior 2	Number of pages	32 pages organized in 4 × 8 pages over the signatures
	Colours	2/2
	Paper	Gloss coated 100gsm
Interior 3	Number of pages	16
	Colours	1/1
	Paper	mass-dyed 120gsm (colour reference tbc)
Finishing	Sewn signatures, board 3 mm/⅛ in, head and tail bands, perfect bound	

Cover	Colours	4/4
	Paper	Gloss coated 135gsm
	Laminate	gloss
Variant	Colours	no
	Real cloth	Red cloth (supply us with colour swatch)
	Laminate	no
	Hot stamp on the front cover board and spine	

Endpapers	Colours	1/1 Pantone
	Paper	Uncoated 140gsm

OPTIONS		
Half-jacket	Colours	4/4
Height 14 cm	Paper	Glossy coated 150gsm
Flaps 10 cm	Laminate	Gloss
		Gold hot stamp on front cover board
	Insert ribbon marker (reference tbc)	

For the 500 copies in English		
Presentation box	Colours	4/4
Board 2.5 mm/⅛ in	Paper	Glossy coated 135gsm
	Laminate	Gloss

Packaging	Shrink-wrapped per unit, in cardboard boxes 10 kg/22 lb maximum, on EPAL pallets
	Stick a reference sticker supplied by us on the boxes

Shipping	1,000 copies FR: two points in Greater Paris (warehouse), 300 copies Fontainebleau (tail lift and pallet jack)
	500 copies UK: one point Greater London (warehouse), 100 copies central London (tail lift and pallet jack)

Terms and conditions of payment	tbc

Be precise and thorough. By being disciplined you find out what you don't know about specific subjects: you then ask the right questions at the right time and learn a lot very quickly. Take a cool-headed approach as an apprentice production manager and maintain a constructive dialogue with your service providers.

Checklist
FIND THE RIGHT PEOPLE

- **Set priorities (quality/price/deadlines/proximity/service).**
- **Choose the service providers.**
- **Discuss with service providers.**
- **Compare quotes, negotiate.**
- **Do costings for each item and each job.**
- **Define everyone's role (who does what).**
- **Choose a type of printing.**
- **Stick to the schedules.**
- **Stick to what has been agreed.**
- **Manage conflicts.**

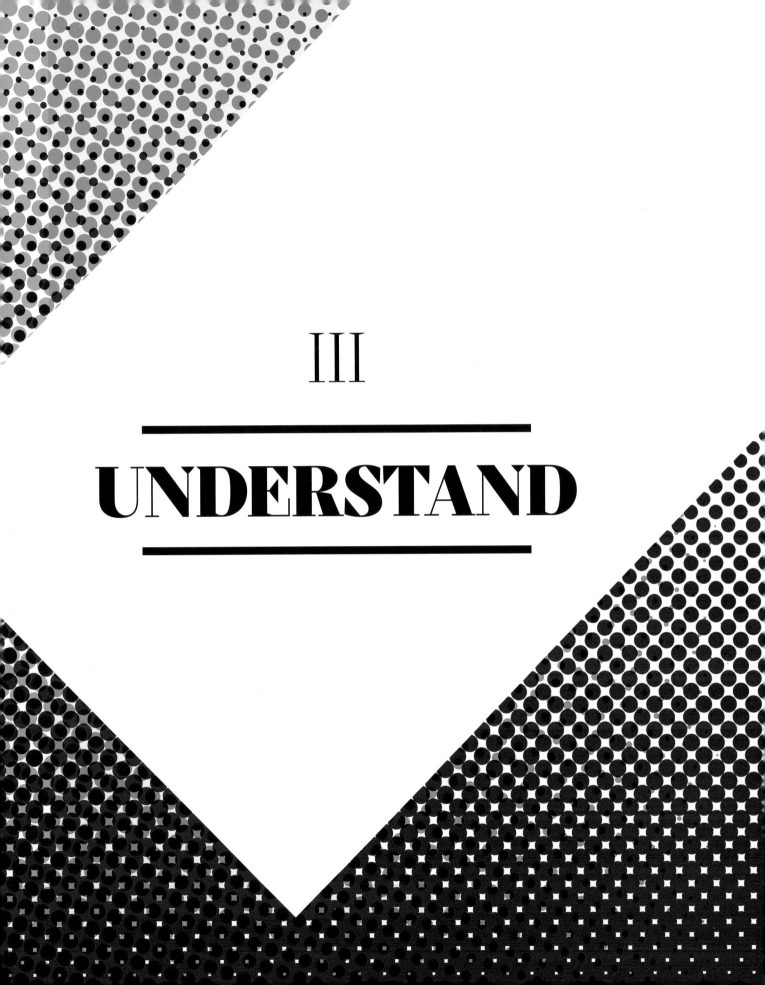

III

UNDERSTAND

If the shade of lipstick or the colour of the trainers you bought online isn't what you expected, the only thing you can blame is your screen and the way it interpreted the colour. When we exchange information solely through screens using the RGB model, we have no grounds to contest or dispute the colour accuracy of a product or artwork; there is often a huge difference in the calibration of monitors, and this is something we cannot currently control. It's only when we transpose images onto an opaque substrate (paper, fabric, metal, plastic) that older and relatively complex rules apply, thus allowing us to share more coherently **this often misleading and subjective perception of colour.**

When we print, we *reproduce*. In other words, we produce something again using means other than our vision. We move from physics to chemistry: it's no longer waves crossing our visual field, but ink and paper molecules coming together. The resulting colour is a new reality whose job is to reproduce reality as closely as possible.

Producing a printed object means understanding the synergy between colour, printing and paper (or any other printed substrate). It's like dancing a waltz: to avoid any missteps and keep to the rhythm and harmony, you need to understand the 'musical scales' of the visual sphere, i.e. the set of rules that governs it. We give detailed explanations in the following chapters.

Colour and images

Light

The sun emits rays of different wavelengths; the Earth's atmosphere filters the ultraviolets and the infrareds, and defuses a white light, which is what we perceive. **The spectrum visible to humans emerges from the separation of this white light.** Although science is evolving in the way it describes this phenomenon, it is usually represented by a prism from which seven groups of wavelengths emerge (see below).

The visible wavelengths range from approximately 400 to 750 nanometres. Before 400 nm are the ultraviolets. After 750 nm are the infrareds. There is an almost infinite number of colours between these two extremes: how many depends on how narrow or how wide the frequency band that we consider a 'colour' is. Scientists often talk about 'monochromatic light' when referring to the light emitted by a single body in fusion: this is often a very narrow band in the light spectrum. In the world of printing, we generally work with the major wavelength groups corresponding to the seven well-known colours of the rainbow.

Newton's prism, or separation of the white light spectrum into seven wavelengths.

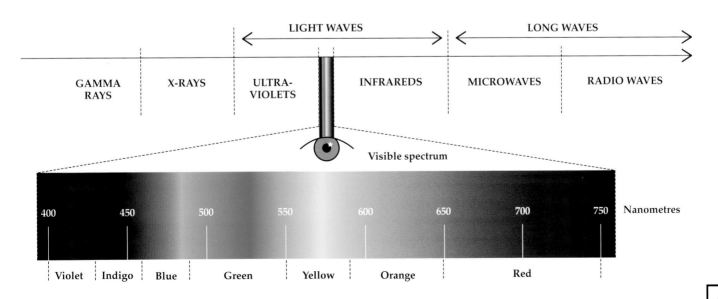

LIGHT WAVES		LONG WAVES	
GAMMA RAYS	X-RAYS	ULTRA-VIOLETS	INFRAREDS	MICROWAVES	RADIO WAVES

Visible spectrum

400   450   500   550   600   650   700   750   Nanometres

Violet   Indigo   Blue   Green   Yellow   Orange   Red

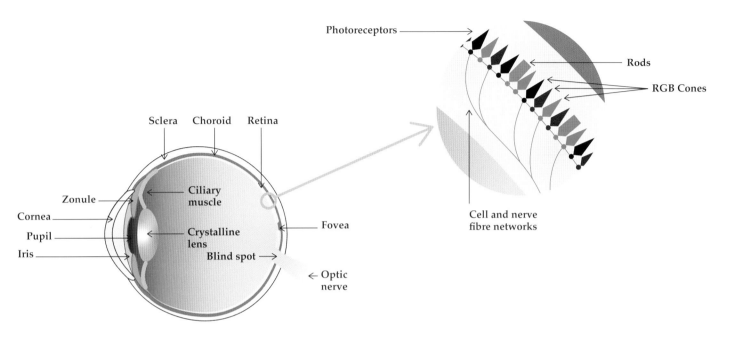

Colour is therefore sensation, not matter. Light stimulates certain photoreceptor cells on the retina, which transform it into a nerve signal. The human eye has two types of receptors: rods, which enable nocturnal vision through contrast and luminosity, and cones, which have photoreceptor pigments that are sensitive to the three groups of wavelengths normally identified as the three primary colours of red/green/blue (RGB). These three groups result from the spectral separation of white light known as 'daylight'. This is the light under which graphics professionals work. It has a temperature of 5500° K (9440° F), which corresponds approximately to the light of the sun at its highest in a sky completely covered with white clouds; i.e., without dominant blues or oranges.

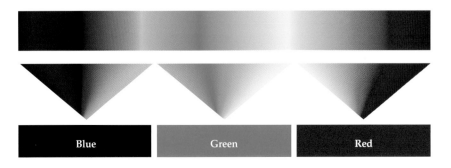

COLOUR IS A FICTION

Blood red, fire red, Ferrari red…
Ultramarine blue, duck egg blue, Klein blue…
Naples yellow, lemon yellow, straw yellow…
The list goes on and on, and the wonderful world of colours deserves an encyclopaedia all of its own. The simple act of talking about colour entails a vocabulary that is as wide-ranging and imaginative as that used by oenologists or perfume makers.

When my grandmother wanted to describe a colour that was insipid and ill-defined, between grey, beige and brown, a colour that changed with the light and was unappealing (in other words, a colour she didn't like), she used to say 'the colour of a rat fleeing'. I'm still looking for it.

An egg yolk is red rather than yellow in my mother tongue of Italian (*il rosso dell'uovo*). You'll notice that white wine tends to be yellowish in real life, whereas in *The Odyssey* Homer often refers to a 'wine-dark sea'. Was the wine of the ancient Greeks a darker, colder tone than our reds? Who knows? In any case, Michel Pastoureau, writing about the history of colours, tells us the Greeks considered blue a barbaric colour, and we only have the Arabic azu(r) or the Germanic root blau/blue to designate the colour blue in Latin languages.

Describing a colour is complex because it is associated with a whole array of sociocultural and emotional beliefs that make us who we are.

The Inuit have a lexicon with dozens of terms for snow and just as many to define the many shades of the colour white, undoubtedly related to their capacity to survive in a world of eternal snow. Meanwhile, many Westerners often use only a handful of vague expressions (off-white, ivory, eggshell) to talk about different shades of white, and we have to make do with the tenuous concept of 'white point' when we talk about paper and colour calibration.

In fact, we could say that colours don't even exist. They are not a tangible reality in the world of physics where waves, particles and molecules drift around in silence. Some scientists even hypothesize that the *perception* (hang on to that word) of colour, sound and taste is a trick our brain plays to survive in the dreary and depressing expanses of the physical universe.

A sound has no physical consistency: it is a wave that hits the eardrum, which sends a vibration to the brain that the latter interprets as being a voice, a noise, a piece of music. A sound emitted from a mountain can even rebound in space (echo), while a sound produced in water will be conveyed with a very particular *muted* note.

The same is true of colours, as they don't exist beyond the light that circulates everywhere in the universe but takes on this specific appearance inside the Earth's atmosphere.

Colours exist only in our heads, in the same way as the words for talking about colour and the attendant emotions exist only in our different cultures, as we have just seen.

In her book, *La Naissance du vert* (The Birth of Green), the artist Anne-Lise Broyer perfectly illustrates the popular French adage 'At night, all cats are grey': colour emerges from the monochrome nocturnal universe as the sun's rays appear at dawn.

The perception of colour

The colour perceived by the eye is **what emerges when light meets a body through which it is reflected or absorbed to a greater or lesser degree**, depending on the nature of the body.

The red of a nail varnish or the bodywork of a Ferrari gives off a much greater vibration than the same shade of red on a piece of velvet or on rose petals in a garden. If you put silk and loose-weave linen in the same washing machine with the same fabric dye, the two fabrics won't have the same brightness or density when you take them out. Similarly, the same inks used on an offset press have very different results on glossy than on uncoated paper, where the lack of coating allows the ink (and light along with it) to penetrate more deeply into the fibres.

In order to grasp the difficulty of reproducing colours on a printed substrate, you need to understand this: on the one hand, there is light, which is an objective physical datum, and on the other, colour, which is the expression of the interaction between light and the medium that emits it (a screen) or reflects it (any surface, including paper).

IT'S ALL RELATIVE: COLOURS ONLY EXIST IN THE HEAD, BUT IT DEPENDS WHOSE

Stop saying 'I see red' when you feel angry like a bull in a ring: a bull sees only grey and his agitation is due to the movement, not the colour, of the fabric. Each species has developed the kind of vision it needs to survive in a given environment; early humans looked for red berries in green bushes and our vision is mainly focused on these colours, while insects search for pollen in the pistils of flowers, so they perceive fluorescent tones. Although insects and spiders are able to perceive ultraviolet rays, the optical spectrum for the majority of animals remains below the electromagnetic spectrum. *Homo sapiens* has three cone types, and is predominantly trichromatic; reptiles and birds have four cone types and see many more shades of colour; dogs and nocturnal mammals are bichromatic and perceive noticeably fewer colours, tending instead to see contrasts (which is also the case for some colour-blind humans); finally, some people suffer from achromatopsia, which is when pigments atrophy in the retina and only the rods are used for vision. But instead of making objects look flat and grey, they appear full of light, like molten metal.

 A screen has a display capacity of 16 million colours, far exceeding our human capacity to distinguish colours. The human eye sees between one and four million colours.

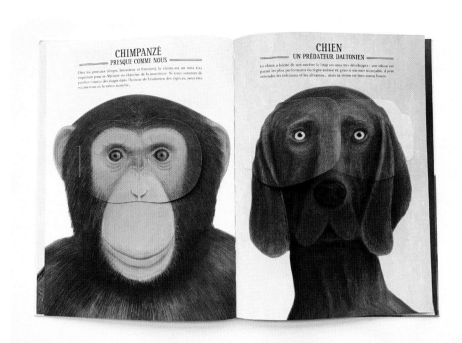

Different vision of different mammals: primates perceive a more extensive colour range than predatory species. Illustration taken from *Zooptique* by Guillaume Duprat, Le Seuil Jeunesse, 2013.

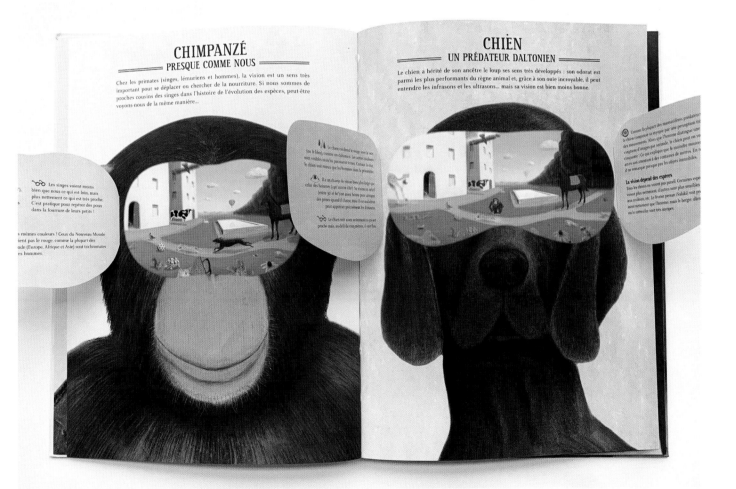

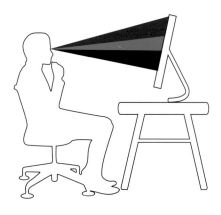

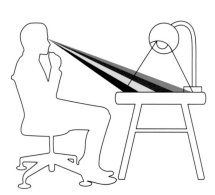

The language of colours has two dialects: that of screens, which emit in RGB (red/green/blue) and that of paper printed in CMYK (cyan/magenta/yellow/key – black). Very different things happen depending on whether a colour is rendered by a light source or reproduced on a printed substrate.

Going from one to the other requires conversion, and that is a profession in itself.

This conversion is not only subject to physical, physiological and cultural conditions, but also involves subjectivity as well as our own professional and emotional concerns. Birth announcement cards made from a photo of your baby taken on your smartphone, the programme for your local kite festival or the book about the 150th anniversary of the company where you're the communications manager are all emotionally charged issues; in each case, you will be aiming for perfection.

The paradox that lies at the heart of graphic production is **the fundamental impossibility of reproducing all the colours visible to the human eye**. Reproducing a colour becomes the art of working with objective and measurable parameters to reconstruct something that is as close as possible to your subjective vision, which itself is determined by a number of universal, personal and cultural factors.

Reputable professionals you work with will tell you that it is impossible to reproduce a colour identical to the rose in your garden. Instead, they will do everything possible to produce the best possible result for you. This brings us back to the keyword in your relationship with the specialists you work with: trust.

See and print a colour

We've seen that the absence of light is black and that the sum of all the wavelengths is white light. The LAB colour space between infrared and ultraviolet covers the spectrum visible to the human eye.

The Atlas of the Munsell describes the way in which visible wavelengths interact according to three parameters: **hue (basic colour), value (lightness) and chroma (colour intensity). This is where all shades of colour are formed, in a manner of speaking.**

By varying the brightness and saturation of each hue that exists in this space, we obtain a theoretical palette of eight million colours visible to humans. In reality, the count is somewhere between one and four million because we are very rarely equally efficient in each RGB channel.

The principle of **additive colour** is the rule that applies when light and the resulting colour are emitted by a light source that strikes the eye directly. 0% light = black; 100% R + G + B = white.

In fact, all light that reaches the eye can be envisaged as an addition of light waves. So, for the retina and its photoreceptors, it can be considered an additive colour.

It's also worth remembering that, except on a screen calibrated to daylight (5500° K/9440° F), white is never an absolute white. Instead it is the reality of the substrate itself: fabric, paper or another surface whose white properties are already colour data in themselves. The **white point** is therefore the fourth essential parameter for dealing with colour in the RGB workspace. Measuring the white point is one of the basic settings done by repro specialists before they tackle the issue of colour characteristics; it is a benchmark of sorts. The gamut (palette) of the RGB space renders only 70% of the visible spectrum, but that's still a lot when you realize that an RGB monitor reproduces 16.7 million colours – four to eight times more than our human vision allows us to see.

Radiation is *emitted* by a bright screen, but *absorbed* by a printed surface. When colour reaches our eye via an opaque surface rather than a screen, the material of the surface absorbs part of the incident light and our eye perceives the residual light reflected by this surface. This is the principle of **subtractive colour**: some of the wavelengths are absorbed by the coloured surface and thus subtracted from the ambient light.

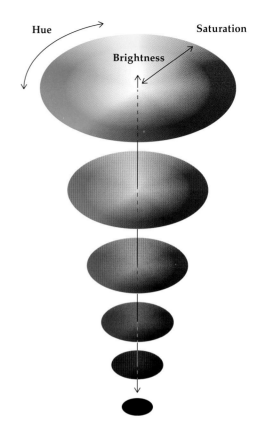

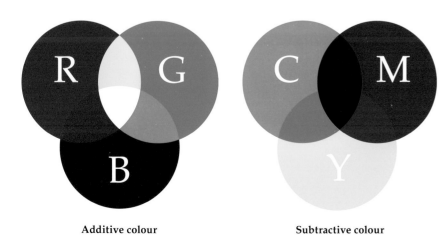

Additive colour   Subtractive colour

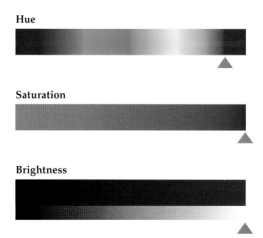

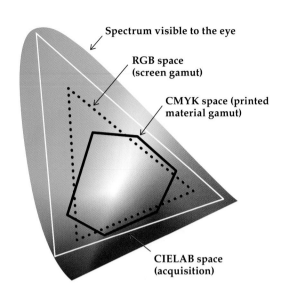

Spectrum visible to the eye

RGB space (screen gamut)

CMYK space (printed material gamut)

CIELAB space (acquisition)

Subtractive colour is about mixing colourants (printing inks, gouache, paint, pigments) rather than emitting light. The more colourants we put in, the more they are absorbed by the substrate, the more reflected light is subtracted and the smaller the re-emitted light spectrum becomes. This subtractive CMYK space of printed matter is another constraint compared to the additive RGB space of screens, of which it is part. This common RGB / CMYK space varies hugely in quality and quantity depending on the type of printing and the paper stock; it determines how well colours are reproduced.

For the human eye, the secondary colours in additive colour (yellow, magenta and cyan, obtained by adding red + green, red + blue and green + blue light, respectively) correspond approximately to the same colours as the three primary colour inks used for printing in subtractive colour. Hence, the sum of the three CMY primary inks gives black by subtracting the transmitted light, while 'white' corresponds to the absence of colourant on a neutral non-coloured substrate.

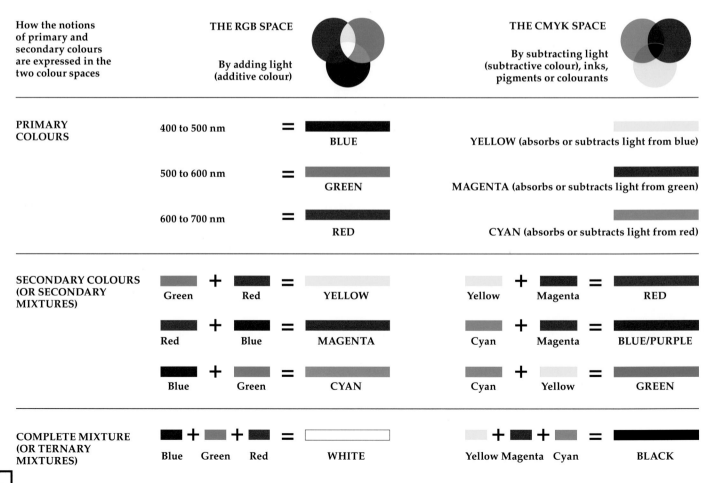

How the notions of primary and secondary colours are expressed in the two colour spaces	THE RGB SPACE By adding light (additive colour)	THE CMYK SPACE By subtracting light (subtractive colour), inks, pigments or colourants
PRIMARY COLOURS	400 to 500 nm = BLUE	YELLOW (absorbs or subtracts light from blue)
	500 to 600 nm = GREEN	MAGENTA (absorbs or subtracts light from green)
	600 to 700 nm = RED	CYAN (absorbs or subtracts light from red)
SECONDARY COLOURS (OR SECONDARY MIXTURES)	Green + Red = YELLOW	Yellow + Magenta = RED
	Red + Blue = MAGENTA	Cyan + Magenta = BLUE/PURPLE
	Blue + Green = CYAN	Cyan + Yellow = GREEN
COMPLETE MIXTURE (OR TERNARY MIXTURES)	Blue + Green + Red = WHITE	Yellow + Magenta + Cyan = BLACK

Be aware, however, that the black obtained by superimposing the three inks/primary colours is really just a dark grey-brown. **A black ink has therefore been added to this new colour space to ensure sufficient density and opacity.**

+

+

=

OPACITY AND DENSITY

For opaque documents like printed matter and photographic prints, opacity is the relationship between incident and reflected light. Similarly, for transparent documents such as film it is the relationship between incident and transmitted light.

In film photography, this would correspond to the opacity of the film.

In printing and photogravure, density is an important concept. It's a way of measuring the opacity of a print.

Opacity = incident light/retransmitted light (there is no unit for this value).

Density (D) is the common logarithm (log10) of opacity.

The densitometer is an indispensable tool when producing printed materials. It compares the brightness of an incident light, emitted by a lamp, with the brightness retransmitted by the sample being measured.

This simple relationship between these two quantities of light is called opacity, and is directly converted and displayed as density by these devices.

In printing, all densities of black and coloured inks need to be checked. To measure the latter, a coloured filter of complementary colour is placed in front of the incident light to calibrate the densitometer's reference 'white'.

+

=

BANANA SKIN

Setting and using the right profile is essential. By now, you'll have realized that you can't process any image file without having fully decided which material you are going to print on. Paper is not the only option. You may want to print on metal, stone, fabric or even vinyl. If you supply a file designed for a material other than the one you will be printing on, you may get a nasty shock when it comes to the colour rendering and density.

Converting RGB to CMYK almost halves the colour gamut (range), and is asymmetrical because the two spaces do not fully coincide. Some colours that look very saturated and bright on the screen can never be fully rendered by inks on an opaque substrate such as paper, however glossy and coated it is. This is the first pitfall of colour reproduction. **The other problem is that each device in the production chain renders colours in a different way.** Therefore, in order to guarantee reproducibility when switching from one device and one palette to another, highly specific workspaces have been defined for each palette and **conventions established to make these switches reliable, constant and predictable**.

The International Colour Consortium (ICC) has established standards or criteria for creating ICC profiles. **A profile is a calibration tool**. This is a file that contains information on each device's characteristics and its specific gamut (its 'colour identity card'), which makes it possible to adapt all variables to a single standard. It is a standard, theoretical space called the CIELAB space – the visible spectrum between infrared and ultraviolet. Let's look at the two major categories that are most often used:

– **ICC profile for coated paper**: white glossy coated paper with a maximum ink coverage of 300–350%, which permits high densities and colour strengths: FOGRA 39L > 51L.

WHICH STANDARD FOR WHICH PAPER STOCK?

The CMYK workspace is defined based on offset printing on white paper with a given quantity of ink according to the paper type.

Professional organizations, such as FOGRA in Europe and Asia, and SWOP and GRACoL in the US, publish charts based on a printing-specific international ISO standard. These charts contain average measurements taken from a wide palette of colours printed on the same paper using different machines.

There is therefore a FOGRA standard for each type of substrate: matt or glossy coated, lick coating, uncoated, very white or slightly cream, matt or glossy laminated. All these types of paper absorb ink in different ways and therefore reflect the light and colour that we visually perceive in different ways.

– ICC profile for uncoated (offset) paper: uncoated white paper with 270% ink coverage, which permits much lower densities and colour strengths: FOGRA 47L > 52L (see opposite).

The material and its capacity to absorb or reflect light therefore dictates the technology and consequently the profile to adopt.

So the key question is: what type of file for what type of printing and on what type of material?

If you are developing the same visual for a range of variants, you need to create different files and specific curves for each material and each printing technique (digital, offset, gravure, flexography).

In effect, this means you need to be careful with compensation curves when the same visual is used for different outputs. If you are a novice in this technique, it is strongly recommended to work with a prepress specialist. In most circumstances, you would be working with a repro house and using a particular profile such as 51L or 52L to output files correctly for printing.

Images and colour on the screen

Digital image: this is a binary file, i.e., in a language composed of sequences of ones and zeros in different combinations that generate information whose basic unit is the bit (0 or 1) and that is usually measured in octets (or bytes) or their multiples (MB, megabytes, or GB, gigabytes).

A digital image is:

– acquired via a scanner or a camera,

– created using software,

– corrected, retouched in repro,

– stored.

Visualizing a pixel on a computer screen.

Pixel: (short for picture element): this is the smallest visual item in a digital image or on a screen where it is displayed.

A screen pixel is a different concept from an image pixel. For example, one image pixel can be several pixels on a screen, or vice versa.

A pixel in a digital image is a purely computer-based entity composed of a minimum of the three component values: red, green and blue. In this case, a pixel is the smallest detail in the image.

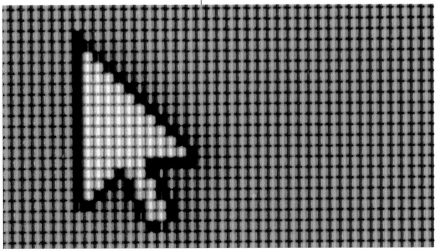

Excessive enlargement of a greyscale image causes its components, pixels, to become visible, whereas a vector image does not have the same limitations and can be enlarged at will.

A pixel on a screen is a unit of physical surface consisting of three phosphor dots or RGB bars: red, green and blue. This physical surface is connected to the screen definition when it is designed and manufactured; it is measured in micrometres (µm).

The definition of an image is the total number of pixels that compose it. For example: an image that is 2,000 pixels high and 4,000 pixels wide has a resolution (in other words, size) of 2,000 p × 4,000 p, or eight million pixels. This number remains the same when the image is reduced or enlarged without being resampled: the result will be a lower- or higher-resolution image.

You need to plan for sufficient resolution right from the start if you want good definition, because this determines the information density of the image and defines its potential. **If the initial resolution is low, the definition will be mediocre**; it will become downright awful if the image is enlarged, because enlarging the surface increases only the size, not the number of pixels. This makes them visible to the naked eye and the effect is known as pixelation (or low resolution).
Vector images (computer-generated images such as drawings, logos, barcodes) **consist of lines, curves and points** (vectors) or mathematical formulae rather than pixels. They can be enlarged at will as they have no resolution of their own until resolution is applied for printing via printing line screen.

Resampling The concepts of resizing and resampling an image should not be confused: the first is changing the dimensions while keeping the

BANANA SKIN

While it's easy to understand that over-enlarging can compromise image definition, we tend to imagine that doing the opposite is not a problem and that we can reduce the size of a file as much as we want. But be careful! If your image is dark, you risk losing detail on the printed sheet, because too many ink dots will be called into service for too great a concentration of information in the file. Sometimes it's better to rework an image that is heavily reduced in size: resample it, slightly desaturate it and 'open up' the highlights. The best method is to reduce it in Photoshop and import the new image into InDesign, or get your repro house to make the necessary adjustments.

same number of pixels, whereas the second is changing both the size and the resolution by recalculating the number of pixels in Photoshop, which reinterprets the information to better adapt it to the use required. If you decide to reduce or enlarge an image by resampling, what you actually do is 'create' or 'destroy' pixels from the original file so that the image becomes the size the operator requires, but the image obtained will not have the same number of pixels as before. This can quite often destroy details and should only be performed if you know what you are seeking to achieve.

PPI This is the number of pixels per inch. The generic word dot, sometimes used to designate a pixel, should not be confused with a printable dot, which is found in the acronym DPI explained on page 60.

The greater the concentration of pixels, i.e., **the more of them in a file, the more information there will be**, generating better detail and colour reproduction in a printed image.

Capture/restitution Generally speaking, we tend to work with digital images whose definition is linked to a camera. In other cases, you need to scan documents, and the scanner operator will set a particular resolution based on the planned output format. We talk about capture resolution to describe the capacity and the setting used on a digital camera sensor or to describe the parameters used on a scanner when scanning an analogue document.

Before you scan a document, you therefore need to know the print size for your illustration.

You should always keep the output format in mind. A double-page spread in a magazine cannot be reproduced from a thumbnail image (i.e., the same format as the scanned object), because the input resolution will not be sufficiently scalable.

Once the input resolution has been defined, you'll have some leeway and be able to increase the size of your image a little. Tolerance is generally around 30%, but you can sometimes go beyond this if your initial file quality is satisfactory or if you don't require a perfectly sharp reproduction. The maximum resolution for different ranges of cameras is known.

THE AWKWARD QUESTION

To do things properly, do you always need to acquire an image in the highest resolution possible?

No. Although the original resolution is a determining factor for the future definition of the image to be printed, too high a resolution leads to an unnecessarily large file that makes the layout file bigger and slows down the viewing and printing on an office printer. Use the best resolution appropriate for the printing output. To be safe, it is usually a good idea to work to a resolution a bit higher than you expect to need, so the question should always be: 'what is the next step?'

The more you increase the physical size of an image, the more you dilute the concentration and size of the pixels. It's like pulling on a fishing net… or fishnet stockings!

Scanners have variable resolution that can achieve very high quality. However, the higher the resolution required, the longer the acquisition takes and the more your supplier may charge for the service. But sometimes it is worthwhile, or even unavoidable, to spend a little more to have more wiggle room later.

If you're working on the cover of a 20 × 30 cm/8 × 11 in exhibition catalogue and you already know that the chosen visual will be used for 40 × 60 cm/15 × 24 in posters, you might as well start directly with 600 DPI (see below) for the cover. When the image is scaled up to its usable size, you double the output size for the poster; this halves the definition (PPI), but in the end you still have the 300 DPI resolution needed for good offset reproduction. In this case, there is no resampling, because there is no recalculation of pixels, just a change of image size.

Images and colour on paper

Things get a bit more complicated when we leave the ethereal universe of the binary system and get our hands dirty at the printing press.

DPI When we print an image we usually express resolution as DPI (dots per inch) because we print in dots rather than pixels. These dots are configured and profiled according to the chosen type of printing. Laser printers use toner dots, inkjet printers use specific inks, and sheet-fed and web offset presses use dots of oil-based ink that are transferred to the paper from a screen grid that can be measured in DPI.

Although most monitors now are around 100 to 200 DPI (and retina screens 300+ DPI), a computer screen can reproduce an image of acceptable quality with a resolution of only 72 DPI (100 DPI for a responsive file – a format that can be adapted to smartphone screens), but on paper,

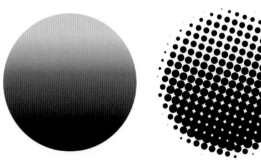

Value

Definition

Black 40%
screen 60 lines
per inch

Black 40%
screen 100 lines
per inch

Black 40%
screen 150 lines
per inch

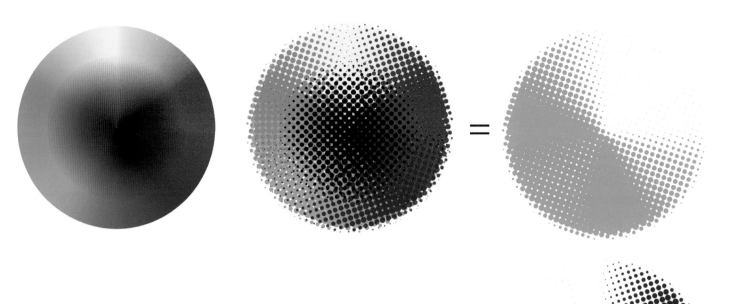

you need a resolution of at least 150 DPI for laser printing, 200 DPI for digital printing and 300 DPI for offset and photogravure printing. Vector or line drawings do not have their own resolution and will need an image setter resolution of at least 1200 DPI to get the most out of them. If you're working on a website and you suddenly need to prepare images for a paper version, and subsequently for a tarpaulin or a window sticker, don't forget this requirement, otherwise you'll end up with embarrassingly pixelated low-definition images in your printed document and files that aren't suitable for large-format digital printing.

<u>Screening</u> Whenever you have offset printing, you also have screening. If you look closely at a poster in the underground, or whenever you look at any printed image through a magnifying glass, you'll notice that the image isn't as smooth and uniform as your eyes see it when you're the right distance away. **You can see lots of coloured dots that are generally arranged geometrically.**

Unlike a continuous tone (of a photo print, a transparency or a digital image containing millions of pixels), an image reproduced to be printed is a screened image, i.e., it consists of a mesh of closely spaced dots of different shapes and sizes. These dots are arranged in a varying number of lines, and they reproduce the image as four different halftones, one per colour and per plate. And they do this for each of the three primary colours and black with different gradations (shades of grey). The superimposition of these four halftones ensures that the inks are mixed in different proportions and allows a large number of visible colours to be reproduced.

Below, detail of a 4 × 6 poster as seen by the naked eye. On the left, the detail is dramatically enlarged: the printing line screen is clearly visible.

These dots determine the exact place where the ink will be deposited on the paper; the number, size and shape of these dots will determine how accurate the reproduction is, but the ink is not directly transferred to the paper. We will see how it's done on page 97.

1	2
3	4

On the following double-page spread, we can see how an image behaves on two different paper stocks, according to the process it has undergone, or not, in repro.

In images 1 and 2, we have simply applied the profile for each type of paper: FOGRA 51L for coated paper (image 1), FOGRA 52L for uncoated paper (image 2).
In images 3 and 4, the profiles were applied and colour work was then done to make the two results visually similar.
To give an example, an advertising poster can be printed in offset, digital or photogravure. The basic file is always processed for printing on coated paper. This initial version serves as a reference for any subsequent adaptation for other stock or substrates.

Checklist
UNDERSTAND COLOUR AND IMAGES

Be aware of the colour space you are working in.

Work on colour in cool, neutral light conditions with calibrated devices, and avoid wearing or being surrounded by bright colours when checking.

Base your colour work on the material you will be printing on.

Pay attention to the resolution, definition and enlargement rate of the images.

Plan to resample images that will undergo significant resizing.

Apply or make sure your supplier applies the appropriate profiles (FOGRA standards).

L'épaisseur de la lumière

2

Paper

How paper is made

If you're curious about the subject, there are many books on paper production and the techniques associated with its different uses; here, we'll skip banknotes, cigarette papers and wallpaper, and just touch on a few technical notions to get a better understanding of what we are interested in: how to choose a type of paper to print on and how to finish it correctly for publication.

Paper is basically a pulp made from cellulose that undergoes lengthy processing on a machine the size of a football pitch. Ground wood fibres are mixed with enormous quantities of water (the initial ratio is 1 to 99%), and then laid out in the same direction to form the 'web', a liquid sheet that is sieved, pressed, dried, smoothed, covered in pigments, binders and colourants and possibly coated with a mineral layer. These sheets are then rolled into huge 'mother reels' that are cut into 'daughter reels', and then again into sheets for printing on offset presses.

Paper therefore has a similar structure to fabric. Like fabric, it has a 'direction': the position of the fibres determines how flexible it is when folded and consequently how easy it is to open a brochure or a bound book.

The correct direction of paper, parallel to the long side following the length of the fibres, is called machine or grain direction. When printing, it's best to stick to this direction as much as possible to avoid the pitfalls we'll talk about later (see page 114).

An 'against the grain' paper can cause the block to wave.

The structure and uniformity of the paper can be checked by transparency.

The fibres that make up the pulp come from diverse materials that undergo different processing depending on the result required. Until the nineteenth century, paper pulp was made using fibres from hemp and linen rags (rag paper), and then with cellulose fibres from different types of wood: resinous softwood (pine, fir, etc.) for long fibres that make strong paper, and leafy hardwood (eucalyptus, oak, birch, etc.), whose short fibres make it possible to tweak the quality and the particular character of a paper, its opacity and its structure – in other words, its uniformity visible through transparency.

Pulps are either chemical or mechanical: the latter contain lignin residues that cause paper to yellow and become brittle in the short term. Coated or uncoated papers containing traces of wood therefore tend to be used primarily for magazines and other publications with a short life span, as well as for paperback books. **Chemical pulps produce superior-quality papers**, closer to those previously produced using textiles, where the brown colour of the cellulose has been removed by oxidation, repeated washing and chlorination. **This bleaching process, once highly polluting, is now fairly well controlled**, and high-quality printing papers can now be produced at affordable prices.

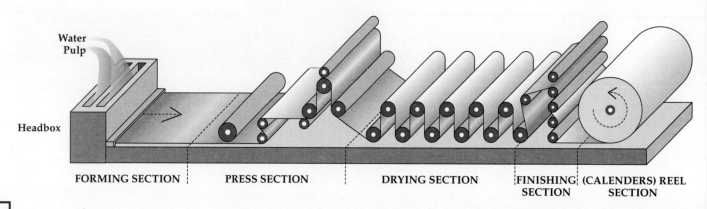

FORMING SECTION | PRESS SECTION | DRYING SECTION | FINISHING SECTION | (CALENDERS) REEL SECTION

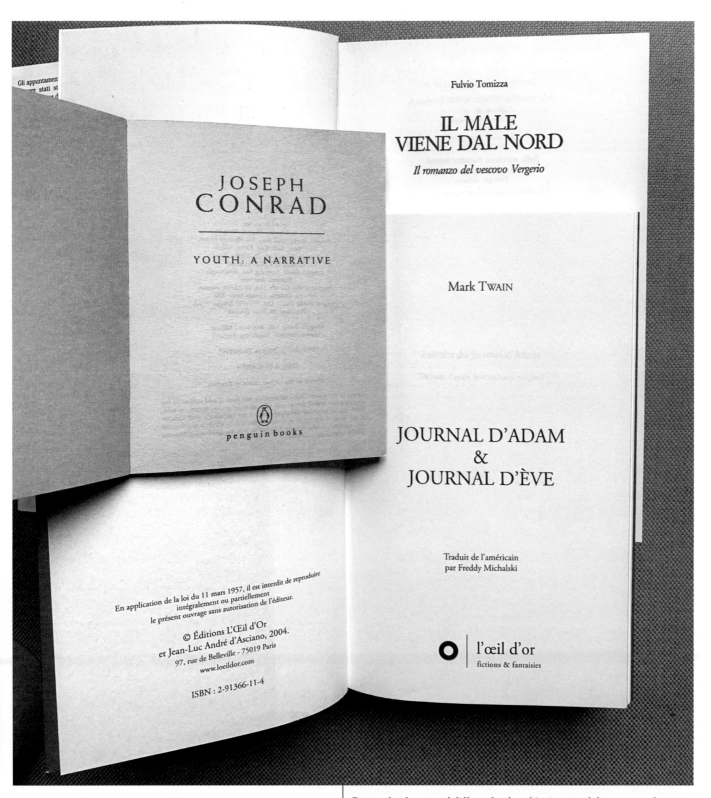

Papers that have aged differently: the white is a wood-free paper, whereas the ivory paper and the cream paper contain varying amounts of lignin (an acid present in wood pulp). The more lignin a paper contains, the more likely it is to yellow over time. A 'wood-free' paper is one in which chemicals have been used to remove the lignin from the wood fibres.

A BRIEF WORLD HISTORY OF PRINTED MATERIALS

The word paper is derived from the Latin *papyrus* and the ancient Greek *pápyros*. It is a durable medium that allowed *Homo sapiens* to externalize, store and consequently expand their memory, initially by recording accounting, legal and notarial acts, and subsequently their stories, beliefs and the accompanying images.

Paper evolved in many ways, and served the cause of the major monotheistic religions, whose respective holy books would be widely distributed. It then underwent its own industrial revolution and ultimately revolutionized our way of thinking.

The Egyptians used thin superimposed strips of papyrus stalks to make scrolls that were used throughout the Mediterranean. But with the fall of the Roman Empire, wars and trade disruptions cut off supplies to Western Europe, and so papyrus was replaced with parchment made from the skins of various herbivores, notably vellum, a particularly delicate but durable process of treating stillborn calf skins that has preserved the brilliance of medieval manuscripts down through the centuries.

In the third century CE the Chinese developed the recipe for modern paper based on bamboo fibres, mulberry bark, and, most importantly, linen and hemp fibres.

This was the beginning of rag paper.

Intense trade between the Persians and the Chinese led to paper circulating around Asia from the sixth century onwards, but it was in the eighth century that the Arabs discovered the secret of paper-making after capturing two Chinese paper-makers at the Battle of Talas. This gave them the technology to accompany their military expansion and to establish the political and religious project of Islam through the transmission of the Qur'an.

As often happened, it was the Arabs who passed on to Christians the best of ancient knowledge and the greatest technological advances, including mathematics and astronomy. As the Arab conquest advanced, paper arrived in Asia Minor, followed by Egypt, Spain and Sicily in around 1000. However, it was in Fabriano, central Italy, that paper production was mechanized in the thirteenth century. From this nerve centre, ideally located between the papal states, the Arab territories to the south, and the north where the bankers and merchant fleets plied their trade across the Adriatic and on to the Mediterranean, paper enjoyed considerable commercial success.

The modern printing press had also emerged in China, Korea and Japan in the form of xylography in the seventh century, and with the invention of movable type in the ninth century, printing was widely used to spread the word of Buddha. In the thirteenth century, something akin to banknotes was printed, and Marco Polo would probably have seen these during his travels. Around the same

Greek papyrus (200 × 295 mm/7¾ × 11½ in), 154 BCE.

It was a Frenchman, Nicolas Robert, who invented a machine to produce paper industrially during the French Revolution, but all subsequent progress occurred mainly in the industrialized Lutheran world. The ever-growing need for supplies led to the end of rag paper and the emergence of a paper-making process (patented in Saxony in 1844) that used pulp based on wood fibres, which were available in huge quantities.

The nineteenth century was the century of the printing press, the pamphlet and the novel. This consumed a lot of paper and required increasingly rapid production methods. Towards the end of the century, the French and subsequently the Italians perfected the principle of letterpress printing by ink transfer, and in 1903, the Americans developed the principle of offset printing.

For six centuries, advancements mostly involved tweaks to the Mainz printing press, but the emergence of computers in the 1970s sped up the process considerably, bringing ever-increasing precision to the reproduction of images on increasingly technical papers.

Printed paper would serve many other causes in very different fields, producing bestsellers ranging from the Bible and the Qur'an to the *Da Vinci Code* and the IKEA catalogue, which finally dethroned the Bible in 2015 with its gigantic global print runs! However, in 2020, IKEA announced it would stop printing its paper catalogue. New era, new values...

time, Genghis Khan's Mongols transported xylographs with them as they built their vast empire.

The future of paper and printing was assured by yet another technological advance that accompanied the emergence of a new church. In the 1450s, Gutenberg perfected the technique of movable metal type, and developed modern typography with printing presses and typographic inks. He printed the Bible, which led to the rapid spread of the teachings of the Reformed Church across northern Europe. But that was not all: over subsequent decades and centuries, the ease of reproducing books led to growth in literacy, popular culture, the development of science, and ideas that circulated more freely.

Example of onion skin paper.

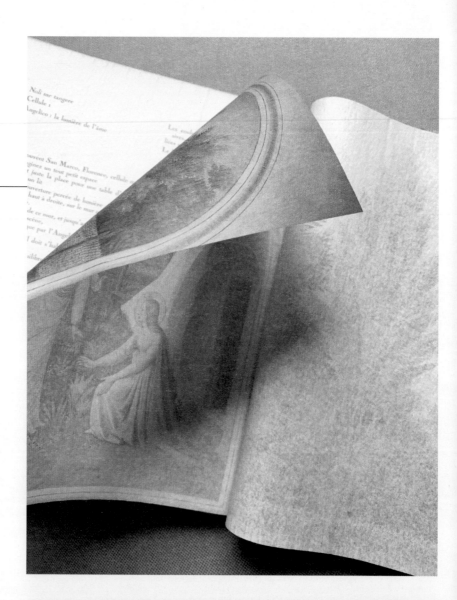

> **✳ TIP**
> **How can you check that your paper is the right and not the 'wrong' (against the grain) way round? If you tear a piece of paper in both directions, you'll see that the tear is cleaner and easier in the direction of the fibres.**

The thinner the paper, the more flexible and cheaper it is, with one notable exception. Flax, hemp and by-products of spinning that would otherwise go to waste are still used to manufacture paper that needs to be extremely thin and strong, such as the paper used in Bibles. This is because these particular fibres are ten times longer than those derived from softwoods. When the grammage of the paper drops below a certain threshold (around 60gsm), you pay more for it because the materials used to make it are now rare and expensive.

Paper and the environment

Contrary to popular belief, **the paper industry, or more accurately the forestry industry, especially in Europe, is one of the most sustainable and least polluting in the world**, unlike industrial farming, intensive livestock breeding or the exploitation of precious raw materials, all of which are responsible for massive deforestation. Wood as a resource, be it for furniture, carpentry or paper, is well managed globally, as Europe and the United States have invested massively in sustainable circular economies.

Paper is displacing plastic in packaging as it is seen as a more environmentally friendly material, and **cellulose pulp production is fast growing and becoming the only alternative to plastic in the packaging sector**.

As paper and cardboard production require considerable quantities of water and energy, the major pulp producers, particularly in northern Europe, are not only managing forestry resources over the long term, but have also become the biggest producers of non-fossil renewable energy, as well as guarantors of clean water, which they scrupulously regenerate. Research and development in this sector takes the long view and the goals are ambitious. It now takes just 4 to 8 m³ of water to make a tonne of paper, compared with 45 m³ in 1980. This is no doubt a result of the fact that many paper mills have become much better at recycling the water they use. (The US benchmark for water use in pulp and paper mills is around 17,000 gallons per ton of paper.)

No, you aren't killing a tree by throwing away a magazine: a tree trunk is used for furniture and timber work, whereas paper pulp comes mainly from sawmill waste or clear-cutting, a common practice in forestry management, as well as from recycled paper and cardboard. Recycling isn't totally carbon-neutral, but the energy balance remains positive, because we can recycle a piece of paper up to seven times. This uses much less water than pulp production. Additionally, the mineral components of coated papers can be recovered for reuse in agriculture.

THE AWKWARD QUESTION

Does printing an email harm the environment?

For a start, we should think twice about sending endless emails with useless attachments and ten people copied in, as that generates ridiculous quantities of digital data that pollute far more than petrol and coal combined. Not to mention our various screens and their non-recyclable components!
The little green tree pictogram makes us think that binning paper equals destroying forests, but we have seen that this is not true. However, printing an email is not good for the environment for one reason: unlike offset inks, which are hydrophobic and therefore can be recovered, toners and other inks used in digital printing and in our home printers are hydrophilic (soluble in water) and disposing of them is always problematic.

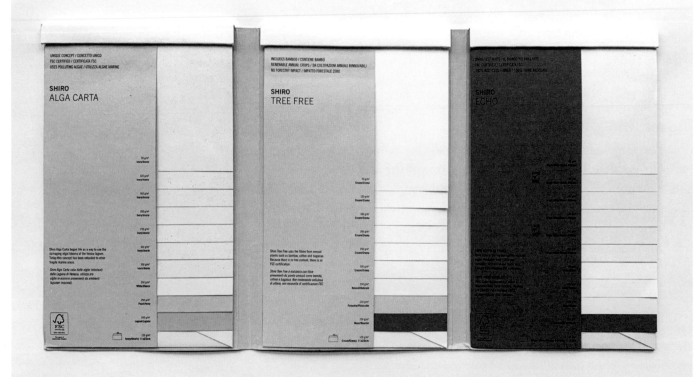

Colour chart of papers made from recycled algae.

GOOD PRACTICE

Algacarta is an example of good practice and inventive longevity in the paper industry. The Italian paper-maker Favini, established in 1736 with the mechanization of rag paper production, has, since 1992, been using excess algae from Venice's lagoon to produce an FSC® certified paper. It proved so successful that, fifteen years later, algae supplies had to be found elsewhere, and Brittany became a major supplier alongside a number of Asian countries. This pretty paper is rather expensive but still affordable and comes in several beautiful shades. And we can assure you it does smell of paper and not seaweed!

It's worth noting that the oil-based inks on recycled paper from traditional printing (photogravure or offset) are recovered using the same principle that applies to printing; these oily, and therefore hydrophobic, inks are separated from the paper in soapy water baths and recovered in the form of sludge, which is then fed into biomass boilers.

Promoting
Sustainable Forest
Management

PEFC/01-00-01   www.pefc.co.uk

Reproduced with the permission of PEFC International

Standards, labels and certifications

Let's not confuse the concepts:

A standard is what guarantees a product's consistent reproducibility and its compliance with stated specifications. It is not related to quality: you can perfectly well print on a non-environmentally friendly product such as plastic, but still adhere to a strict standard.

An environmental standard, however, sets out specific production criteria that take into consideration sustainable management of the planet.

Compliance with these standards, via verification by an organization, leads to certification and a label that defines the properties and qualities of a product or production process.

A printing company can apply for ISO 14001 certification and use these labels subject to an audit by the certifying bodies, which will confirm that the standardized procedures are being followed scrupulously.

In Europe, all paper is produced in an environmentally responsible manner, either using virgin fibres from sustainably managed forests, or derived from recycling, or a combination of the two.

It is possible to go further and demand **certifications that clearly state the composition and give social and economic guarantees in addition to the environmental aspect**.

The FSC® label, which is the most comprehensive and widely used and is managed by an NGO working with Greenpeace and the WWF, takes into account not only an ecosystem's health and biodiversity (like the PEFC label), but also social and legal aspects including the rights of workers in the production chain and the forest rights of indigenous people living in the areas that are being exploited.*

FSC
www.fsc.org

MIX
Paper | Supporting
responsible forestry
FSC® C008047

FSC
www.fsc.org
MIX
Paper | Supporting
responsible forestry
FSC® C008047

How do you choose paper?

Paper is the determining factor that gives a printed object its specific character; **weight, texture, surface and colour convey information and therefore unconscious emotions.**

*For more details on standards and environmental labels, consult FSC.org, PEFC.org or bookchainproject.com.

THE AWKWARD QUESTION

Can you print 100% organic?

Unfortunately not, even if everything possible is being done in the graphics industry to reduce environmental impact – offset printers who obtain ISO certifications for environmental management and no plastics are now legion. Digital printing is not following this example, as we'll see on pages 100 and 103.

Paper exists in different qualities – hard-wearing or less so, smoother or whiter – but what really makes your printed object 'talk' is making sure that the substrate used is appropriate for the subject.

The term 'glossies', applied to magazines from a more carefree era, has since become synonymous with glamour and frivolity. The height of chic in recent years has been to snub this beautiful material and instead print fashion catalogues on uncoated or recycled paper, preferring an environmental and casual feel to reproduction quality, which clearly takes a backseat to the subliminal message.

Let's look at the **three main defining characteristics of paper** in terms of how it behaves in the finishing phase.

<u>**Grammage**</u>, or weight, is mass per square metre (in the US, paper weight is normally measured in pounds). Weight is particularly important when the printed object is sent by post, but other criteria are taken into account in the commercial strategy related to the print substrate: low grammage is always important, but opacity, printability and the lowest possible price are other key criteria for choosing, for example, groundwood, low grammage coated paper for free advertising materials that have a lifespan of a mayfly from your letterbox to your rubbish bin, and are objects for which durability is not an issue.

On other occasions, you may want to add volume to your printed object and will be more interested in two other paper properties:

<u>**Thickness**</u> is the relationship between grammage and bulk. **It's what determines whether or not it is technically feasible to fold** a basic four-page object or a signature consisting of several pages. On a web offset press, for example, it's neither grammage nor bulk, but the thickness of the paper that determines whether inline folding of the signatures is possible. Thickness is measured in micrometres (μm).

<u>**Bulk**</u> is the mathematical relationship between a sheet's thickness and grammage; **a piece of paper has 'bulk' when it appears thicker than its grammage suggests**. It's almost as if we are leaving air between the fibres by adding volume and removing weight. The standard formula for this is: bulk = cm^3/g. In terms of measuring bulk, ordinary coated or calendered uncoated stock has a bulk of 0.7, 0.9 or 1; certain so-called high-bulk matt art papers range from 1.1 to 1.3, and some uncoated papers, that are appropriately called bulky, range from 1.8 to 2. (See page 211 for how to calculate the thickness of a signature according to the grammage and bulk chosen.)

The thickness of a particular paper is related to its grammage but even more so to its bulk.

We can use bulky paper to confer thickness on an object while reducing its weight: with fewer pages and less weight, the buyer feels they have purchased a quality book for a reasonable price. A study carried out in Paris museums confirmed that the biggest buyers of exhibition catalogues are retired people who do not want to carry heavy books around all day.

Finally, it's worth noting that emotions play a major role in the choice of paper. When you're choosing paper for a critical job, don't be intimidated by the complexity but try to explore the different assets and facets of each type of paper: follow your own personal taste and ask your printer for advice. They can advise you on the limitations, advantages and risks of each possible choice.

The different types of paper

We choose paper based on its strength, colour and texture and, primarily, the printing technique used. Price varies according to grammage and technical characteristics.

Each type of paper exists in different grammages.
– 30 to 70gsm: lightweight, technical paper that is often hard-wearing for specific uses (banknotes, bible paper, silk paper, glassine).
– 80 to 170gsm: supple paper for print media and publishing.
– 170 to 300gsm: Semi-rigid paper; from 250gsm and upwards we call it card, coated or uncoated.
– 350 to 400gsm: rigid card, used for packaging, greetings cards, invitations, brochure covers.
– Above this grammage, we call it board and it is no longer measured in weight/m² but in millimetres of thickness.
– For more details, refer to the tables on pages 84 to 86.

Mass-dyed paper, small size,
stored at a printers.

19   22   25   40   14   15   33

Example of speciality paper with
embossing that imitates cloth.

BANANA SKIN

On pages 88 to 91, we discuss
in detail the problem of colour
distortion due to the shade of paper,
but here we simply note that a colour
printed on coloured paper will not
produce the chosen colour, but of
course the sum of the two colours.

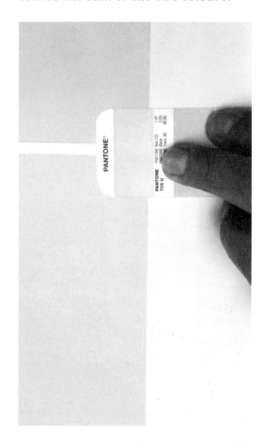

COLOURS AND TEXTURES

Most of the major paper types exist in mass-dyed versions,
which means that the paper is dyed during the reel production
process using pigments or other less polluting processes.
There are also mass-dyed boards.

Semi-rigid cards for covers and packaging, as well as cover
paper for bookbinding, are available with many kinds of
embossing.

The main types of paper

Calendered

The paper is flattened and smoothed to a greater or lesser degree. During production, the sheet is passed through rollers: *kulindros* in Greek. Compression gives it **a certain thickness, opacity and surfacing that limits ink absorption**. The more calendered paper is, the smoother but also the thinner it will be, losing bulk.

Uncoated (Offset)

This is paper that is calendered to a greater or lesser degree depending on the bulk you wish to give it, and the surface is starched to reduce ink penetration. **It was originally designed as a material for reading and writing due to its matt appearance.** Uncoated paper, particularly in the bulky version, is widely used for textbooks.

The type of paper and coating will determine the paper surface and influence the finished printed result.

On the right, a self-portrait by Pablo Picasso printed in 1987 on a semi-matt coated paper; on the left, the same painting reproduced in 2018 on an uncoated paper. Although the legibility of details in the dark areas can be defined by carefully working on the curves, the colour shift is unavoidable because of how different paper stocks absorb ink, affecting dot gain and perceived colour.

NO PAPER CAN ACHIEVE THE IMPOSSIBLE

Despite the undeniable service record of coated paper, uncoated stock has been the trend in publishing for the past fifteen years, including for art books, where faithful reproduction of images is paramount. Huge improvements have been made in the manufacture of these products, and paper manufacturers have boosted sales through extremely costly marketing campaigns. We now have lovely bright colours and great results, but, let's face it, there are details and colours that you will never be able to reproduce on uncoated paper. The laws of optics, probably more resistant to change than those of the market, always govern the behaviour of a colour spectrum on a given material, and there is nothing we can do about it. If a colour specialist sometimes puts the brakes on your ambitious plans, it's because they simply cannot go any further. It's difficult for them to categorically refuse you, and they will do their best to achieve the best possible result given the constraints they are under vis-à-vis the stock that you have chosen to print on.

The same tint printed on satin paper (below) and on high bulk matt art paper (above). The latter is less smooth because it is not as calendered and is more absorbent, which changes the radiance of the colours.

Coated

In addition to calendering, paper can be further processed or given additional finishes to create different appearances; one common finish is a layer of kaolin and other adjuvants, which are either applied to both sides of the paper or just one in the case of one-side coated papers and cards used for posters, book jackets and brochure covers.

Modern coated paper has a single layer, whereas traditional coated paper has a double or even triple layer. This confers the best porosity to receive the ink without it entering the fibres or remaining on the surface, in which case it risks being transferred to the next sheet (set-off). Coated paper is best suited to precise colour rendering, because it reduces the effect of 'dot gain', when the ink spreads out and soaks into the paper. As the ink remains on the surface, light tends to be reflected rather than absorbed, allowing the colour spectrum to be expressed to the full.

Depending on whether the paper has been more or less calendered and whether it has had one or several layers added, it will be glossy, semi-matt or matt: the shinier it is, the less bulk it has and vice versa. A glossy paper will be seen as soft in comparison with matt or semi-matt stock of the same grammage, which is thicker and firmer.

High bulk matt art

This is a hybrid category of paper. It has a very matt appearance and is somewhere between coated and uncoated. It's best to ask the printer to advise on the most appropriate profile to apply. For high bulk papers such as Arctic Volume it is common to use a coated profile, so 51L.

Depending on its surface condition, paper receives ink in different ways, and the colour rendition can be fairly varied. Therefore, care must be taken when processing images because colour has no character of its own – its behaviour is directly related to its capacity to reflect the light that is absorbed by the printed substrate in different degrees.

In the table on pages 84–86, you'll find the main characteristics and the pros and cons of each paper stock and the best FOGRA profile to use with each.

TIP
The best way to choose your paper stock is to get some colour charts from distributors. You can also show your printer a publication that uses the kind of paper you want: they will find the reference or suggest a similar paper. In any case, ask for samples, as your printer can easily get hold of them from paper producers. Asking for a blank mock-up (or white dummy) of your product is strongly recommended, especially for a book that is quite thick. It's only when you hold the object in your hands that you'll be able to feel its substance, how heavy and flexible it is and whether it is easy to open or not.

WHITE SILVER
LIGHT SILVER
LIGHT SILVER
SILVER PIGMENTS
GOLDEN SILVER
AQUA SILVER
BROWN SILVER
BLACK SILVER

bleu acier / flanelle / bleu pâle / bleu pâle / mint / mint / gris perle / gris perle / vert nature / vert nature / citron / citron / chamois / chamois / blanc cassé / extra blanc

www.GMUND.com

g/m²	100 Cult	135 Cult	200 Cult	300 Cult	300 Wild	Envelopes
CHEVREAU	○	•	•	•	•	•
GAZELLE	○	•	•	•	•	•
DAIM	○	•	•	•		
LAMA			•	•	•	•
CAMÉLÉON			•	•	•	•
CROCODILE			•	•	•	•
LÉZARD			•	•	•	•
BOA			•	•	•	

SPECIALITY PAPERS

Transparent, reflective, metallic, embossed, iridescent, grained... There is a vast choice for creative use in sectors such as fashion and graphic design. They can be coated or uncoated, and come in numerous dyed versions as well as a wide variety of textures and interesting kinds of embossing for card and paper designed for binding or packaging.

It's worth noting, however, that these materials are not always intended for the same uses: some are specifically designed for binding and can be used to cover board without 'cracking' on the folds, whereas others can only cope with a simple scoring.

UNCOATED

	BULKY	NEWSPRINT	THIN UNCOATED	UNCOATED
GRAMMAGE	from 45 to 90gsm	from 35 to 60gsm	from 22 to 60gsm	from 60 to 350gsm
BULK	1.5 to 2.2	(variable and non-archival)	1 to 1.2	1 to 1.4
APPEARANCE	Rough, porous, very matt	Smooth, satin in 'supercalender-ed' version	Various: bible paper, onion skin paper, silk paper	Smooth or 'grained'
USE	Textbooks, simple line or greyscale illustrations, watercolours	Daily press, free flyers, directories, only in web (see page 93)	Volumes with very high pagination; very opaque and hard-wearing in relation to weight, used for patterns, liturgical books, dictionaries and directories	Literature, high-quality illustrated books, road maps, office use, press and communication
ADVANTAGES	Thick and lightweight, opaque, perfect for reading and writing; comes in white and ivory, soothing for reading; particularly suited to softcover binding (glued) as glue takes well	Thin, low grammage, opaque, hard-wearing	Paper designed to be hard-wearing and stable for printing	For office use or art books, there are various versions, with different degrees of smoothness and shades of colour; stable when printing, strong, opaque, can be used for four-colour and detail work
DISADVANTAGES	Porous, absorbs ink, not shiny at all, not suited for photos and four-colour in general	Very porous, lacks bulk, rapid yellowing	Expensive as very technical; very difficult to handle when printing and finishing (need to work with specialists)	Rigid in high grammages, lack of coating allows ink to penetrate the fibres despite surface finish: colours are dull and details blurred in the dense tones
PROFILE	FOGRA 47L > FOGRA 52L	FOGRA 47L > FOGRA 52L	FOGRA 47L > FOGRA 52L	FOGRA 47L > FOGRA 52L

COATED

THIN COATED	SHINY COATED	SEMI-MATT COATED	MATT COATED	HIGH BULK MATT ART/VOLUME
from 22 to 60gsm	from 70 to 350gsm	from 70 to 350gsm	from 70 to 350gsm	from 70 to 170gsm
0.75 to 0.8	0.75 to 0.85	0.85 to 0.92	0.9 to 1	1 to 1.3
Smooth	Very smooth and glossy (with sheen)	Smooth and silky	Matt or ultra-matt, smooth	Very matt
Mailings, sales brochures, flyers, mail-order catalogues, (instruction) booklets for various products	Magazines, brochures	Books, magazines, brochures	Books, magazines, brochures	Books, magazines, brochures
Very cheap, very low grammage, quite stable when printing	Good colour rendering, inks stay better on the surface the more coating it has (single, double or triple)	Good bulk, good for printing, good ink absorption, opaque	No shine, so suitable for reading; a good compromise between the opacity of un-coated and the printability of glossy	More volume and less grammage
Apart from illustrated encyclopaedias, it can only be used for bottom-of-the-range, throwaway products; hard to handle in printing and finishing (need to work with specialists)	Highly calendered, it is softer with low bulk; inking tends to crack at the fold in high grammages; not suitable for reading due to shine	Less shine compared to coated glossy	Low calendering, ink may not absorb well (varnish sometimes required); slightly narrower colour spectrum compared to glossy or satin	Duller colours, lower pagination signatures for folding
FOGRA 39L > FOGRA 51L	FOGRA 39L > FOGRA 51L	FOGRA 39L > FOGRA 51L	FOGRA 39L > FOGRA 51L	In principle, FOGRA 39L > FOGRA 51L, but it is recommended to slightly darken the highlights and reduce the three-quarter tones*

* Sometimes, depending on what is being reproduced, an uncoated paper profile may be more appropriate. Consult your printer before you (or someone else) works on the images.

OTHER PAPERS

	KRAFT AND COVER PAPER	COATED CARD	BOARD	DIGITAL PAPER
DESCRIPTION	These are papers made from long fibres extracted from softwood, and are primarily designed to be hard-wearing (kraft paper for packaging, paper for road maps, etc.), and supple (materials to cover boards without cracking at the fold; covers of hardcover books, presentation boxes, cardboard packaging)	Used for packaging or covers of books and brochures, a card can weigh from 250 to 400gsm; it can be uncoated or coated on one side or both sides; speciality card and papers are available in many different kinds of finishing and embossing	Generally designed to be covered in another material (paper, cloth, binding material), board is between 0.5 and 5 mm thick; untreated board is grey but there are mass-dyed versions	These are papers used to print using toners and inkjet; they need to withstand either thermal shocks (drying), or high humidity (inkjet); and consequently undergo special processing; paper-makers increasingly supply digital versions of their ordinary or speciality papers
PROFILE	FOGRA 47L > FOGRA 52L	FOGRA 39L > FOGRA 51L on the coated part, FOGRA 39L > FOGRA 51L on the uncoated part	NB: board is either printed using screen printing or with hot stamping, i.e. graphic line elements (1,200 DPI)	Consult the printer

OTHER SUBSTRATES

	METAL	PVC	GLASS	PERSPEX	TEXTILE	WOOD
PROFILE	FOGRA 39L > 51L	FOGRA 39L > 51L	FOGRA 39L > 51	FOGRA 39L > 51L	FOGRA 47L > 52L	FOGRA 47L > 52L

Here we have listed the most common substrates that can be printed on using various techniques. Technologies evolve very quickly and the information provided here is just to give you an idea, which you would be advised to check. Nearly all these substrates can be printed on using silk-screen and often offset printing, but only if HUV/LED (hybrid UV/ light emitting diode) technology is available.

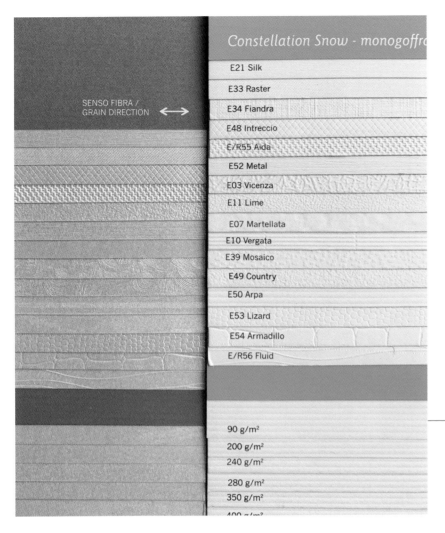

Constellation Snow - monogoffr...

SENSO FIBRA / GRAIN DIRECTION ←→

E21 Silk	
E33 Raster	
E34 Fiandra	
E48 Intreccio	
E/R55 Aida	
E52 Metal	
E03 Vicenza	
E11 Lime	
E07 Martellata	
E10 Vergata	
E39 Mosaico	
E49 Country	
E50 Arpa	
E53 Lizard	
E54 Armadillo	
E/R56 Fluid	

90 g/m²
200 g/m²
240 g/m²
280 g/m²
350 g/m²
400 g/m²

Mass-dyed boards

Coated cards, white or iridescent, with various graining textures.

With the exception of wood and textiles, which tend to absorb inks and for which files need to be prepared as for uncoated stock, most substrates behave like coated paper. However, the resolution and line screen depend on the size of the printed object and especially on the distance from which the object is viewed.

For very large prints, the printable dots are very big, fewer in number and further apart. Images printed in offset on any paper should not be printed below 300 DPI, but 200 DPI is usually sufficient for a shopfront window sticker.

For a plastic tarpaulin, the usual definition is 122 DPI. It can be increased to 200 DPI if you are reproducing a subject that will be looked at closely; it can be reduced to 96 DPI for a very large tarpaulin.

In all cases, the printer can tell you which parameters you need to work with and they will interpret your files and choose the screen for printing. You should therefore contact your printer for each project and ask them what they want to do for a given product on a given substrate.

⚠ *Beware of the printability of certain materials that require special treatment for embossing. Paper manufacturers' colour charts are produced under very specific conditions to achieve the best result, and you cannot be sure that every printer with whatever machine can achieve the same ink penetration on embossed paper.*

White paper and paper whiteness

If you place different sheets of white paper next to each other, you'll quickly see that there can be significant differences in tonality.

Paper whiteness is a subject in its own right that is worth investigating. Depending on the texture and the additives used in the composition of the paper and its coating (if it has one), **the specific tonality of each paper type can vary, and the 'paper white' will be different depending on whether the substrate (paper or something else) is a colder or warmer tone.**
We also know that traces of wood persist in mechanical pulp or ground wood papers, giving a slightly ivory colouring that accentuates over time. In some cases, this warm tone can be used to our advantage in paper for textbooks, because it is calming and conducive to reading. On other occasions, we may be looking for a texture and tonality suitable for drawings, watercolours and pastels, and there are papers specially designed for this aesthetic purpose. What could be better than a slightly ivory bulky paper to reproduce a Leonardo da Vinci drawing?

Elsewhere, we have seen that **one of the most important phases of paper production is when the cellulose pulp is bleached as much as possible** to obtain a good whiteness on the final sheet. That has always been the aim of paper-makers and, until not so long ago, chlorine caused a lot of damage to our rivers.

Cellulose appears yellow because it absorbs waves in the blue range. Just like washing powders, paints, or lotions to make grey hair less yellow, paper is artificially bleached by adding an optical brightening agent (azure > blue > white radiance), a molecule that absorbs ultraviolet radiation (by definition invisible to the human eye) and re-emits it in the form of a bluish-white fluorescence.

When we say that paper is white, we need to agree on exactly which shade of white we mean…

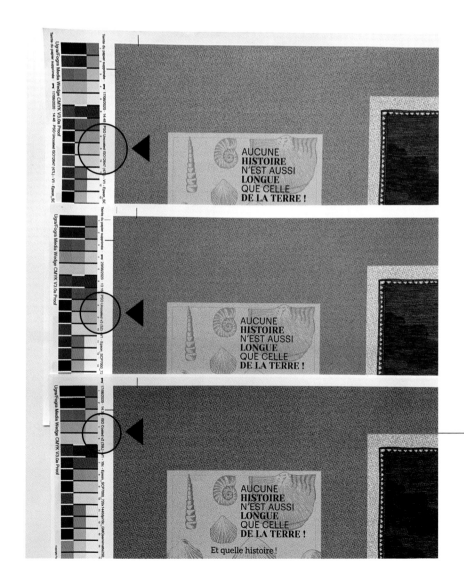

Noticeable colour shifts occur simply by changing the profile, even on the same stock.
From bottom to top:
1) proof with FOGRA 39L profile (coated), satin proof paper;
2) proof with FOGRA 52L profile (uncoated), matt proof paper;
3) proof with FOGRA 47L profile (uncoated), matt proof paper.

On the left, an original on drawing paper; on the right, a 'paper white' scan, which eliminates the colour and grain of the original paper.

Paper and colours

Paper thickness and texture are very variable and the paper interacts with ink (or toner for digital printing) to reproduce colours in different ways. The trend in recent years has been to use very white stock, especially in the uncoated range. It is important to keep in mind that a bright white is in fact a blueish white. When you print colour on it, this needs to be taken into account and managed in the prepress stage, as does the yellow appearance of ground wood papers.

This so-called white paper is what you see in the spaces on your printed sheet, in the 'white', or supposedly white areas (in other words, the parts where there is no ink). 'Scanning to paper white' is an expression used in repro when you need to scan a drawing or a watercolour, for example. This means that if the original watercolour has been produced on slightly coloured drawing paper, the repro professional will set their scanner or image in Photoshop to 'burn out', and therefore not reproduce the printable dots between 0 and 2% that correspond to the shade of paper. This slight percentage of yellow, magenta and sometimes cyan that constitute the colour will be removed so that the image is represented on a perfectly white background.

Nevertheless, don't think that 'scanning to paper white' magically makes specks of dirt and other annoying hickeys on the 'white' edges of the

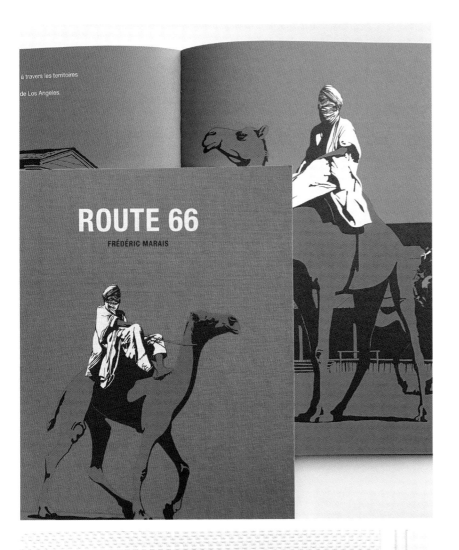

Here is the result of printing on two types of paper with different white points.

The book was printed on a very white uncoated paper and the result is as expected. The cover files (and image) were prepared in the same way as the profile for uncoated paper. However, due to the cover paper having a different white point (off-white and not a pure white), the creamier paper stock has shifted the colour tones.

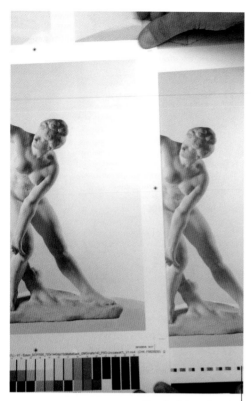

On the left, a digital proof on slightly coloured paper; on the right, an offset print on very white paper: this kind of dramatic colour shift can be surprising, especially for very pale colours.

paper around the illustration or the drawing disappear as if by magic: Photoshop's eraser can take care of those later, but it's an operation that requires time and skill.

Conversely, if you decide to print an illustration on a paper with some colour (some papers from the Arctic range such as Munken Lynx, Gardapat 13, Rives, Conquerors and any other paper that might be called ivory), be aware that **the colours in your illustration will be increased by the density represented by the colour of the paper.**
This stands to reason. If you use navy blue fabric dye on yellow rather than white cotton, you'll end up with bottle green rather than blue fabric when it comes out of the machine.
If you have perfect technical mastery, you know what needs to be done. If not, tell your repro studio which paper you are going to print on. Texture, colour and white point are equally important data.

Checklist
UNDERSTAND PAPER

Determine your priorities for paper:
– grammage (low for sending by post, high for the feel of the object);
– thickness (low to ensure signatures with lots of pages can be folded, high for rigidity);
– bulk (low for a brochure that needs to be flexible, high to achieve volume and lightness).

Check the opacity of the paper, especially for very low grammages and for high bulk papers.

Ask for samples and a blank mock-up/dummy.

Check paper availability with the printer, or production and delivery times.

Order the paper for the planned date.

Choose your paper before starting any colouring operations with either a repro specialist or graphic designer. This is vital.

Inform repro or the designer of the characteristics of your chosen paper (coated or uncoated; very white, white, ivory) so they can adapt the colour matching and apply the appropriate ICC profile. Check the repro proofs are done on stock that simulates your printing stock (coated or uncoated; white point). There is also the option to do wet proofs (or a print test) at the printer using the actual paper chosen for the job, although this will be more expensive.

3

Printing techniques

'To print'… What does the dictionary say? **The act of printing is to mark, to leave a trace** in order to make something appear, whether on a rigid or a soft medium (including the human mind!). It's about exerting pressure on the object to be printed, with or without heat, directly or indirectly. Here, we examine different printing techniques. How do you choose the right one? Most of the time, you don't have a choice: your product dictates the technology. Let's examine the main printing methods.

Web presses

The paper goes into the machine on a reel, is printed on both sides at the same time, then dried in an integrated oven that fixes the ink on the surface. An integrated mechanism then folds the paper and cuts it into signatures corresponding to the preset print form; the assembled set of signatures is then redirected to the appropriate finishing line. There is also the option of finishing directly from the web press by stitching or gluing.

A rotogravure press prints using forms engraved directly on huge metal cylinders, whereas an offset web press prints using plates attached to the cylinders, but the principle of imposition remains the same: the print form is determined by the size of the cylinder or the plate. A form's dimensions are the width of the cylinder, which varies according to the format of the printed object, and the cut-off, which is a fixed length corresponding to the circumference of the cylinder. Paper stock is therefore produced based on these two parameters, of which only the width is variable.

An offset press that has stood the test of time, and still performs well.

Rotogravure press

Unless you have to print the equivalent of *Paris Match* (700,000 copies) or *People* magazine (2,500,000 copies), you will probably never come across rotogravure presses.

We'll skim over this kind of printing: its heyday was the pre-Internet era, especially in the field of mail-order catalogues, now superseded by online versions. **Producing the cylinders and starting up the press, along with the cost of the machine itself, is very expensive and these costs can only be recouped on huge print runs.** You can print a maximum of five colours (four colours + a varnish), with pagination starting from 96 pages per book, on low or very low grammage paper, between 40 and 100gsm.

Web offset press

This uses very hard-wearing plates mounted on cylinders, which reduces costs that are then more quickly recouped. **This technique is suitable for print runs from tens of thousands to hundreds of thousands of copies, depending on the pagination.** It is therefore intended for commercial brochures, flyers, free handouts, ordinary magazines, etc., with pagination from 16 pages per signature, on paper from 40 to 135gsm. As with rotogravure, the fifth colour is usually a varnish: managing a spot colour on a web press requires manual intervention, which negates what we expect from these machines, namely speed.

We can have sheet output from a web offset press; it isn't as fast, but it can handle more complex folding and thicker paper stock. It's good for publications with a large print run (such as school textbooks or comic books). There are also web presses that print in one or two colours only, on paper from 30gsm (what we call bible paper), which is used to print dictionaries, novels and essays, rulebooks, etc.

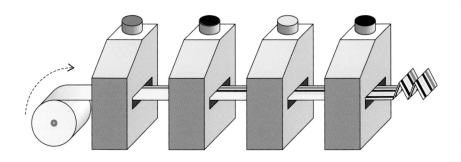

Sheet-fed offset presses

The most common type of offset press uses pre-cut sheets.

Offset is the most flexible system. It can be used to print both small and large print runs and ensure good, or even very high-quality results, at a reasonable cost and using different substrates: a wide range of papers and different grammages, backed fabrics, etc.

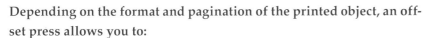

Sheet-fed offset has lower set-up costs than a web press. It prints sheets that are deposited on a pallet at the rear and passed through the assorted units of plates to emerge at the front of the machine, where they are deposited onto other pallets. Once all the forms have been printed, the pallets are transferred to folding machines. These turn the sheets into signatures that are then redirected to the finishing area.

A sheet-fed offset press is slower than a web press, but allows for more precise colour calibration, as each side of the sheet is usually printed separately.*

Depending on the format and pagination of the printed object, an offset press allows you to:

1 — manage print runs ranging from a few hundred to tens of thousands of copies;

2 — print one to ten colours: either the four CMYK primary colours + varnish and/or a spot colour, or four colours + varnish/spot colour on both sides;

3 — use very varied grammages of paper and card from 60 to 500gsm, as well as other materials such as cloth and hybrid materials;

4 — create very varied impositions and therefore highly articulated finishes with combinations of very different signatures, including foldouts, or smaller signatures with a mix of different papers.

*The presses usually have four or five units, but there are some with eight to ten units that can print pages on one side and then the other immediately after.

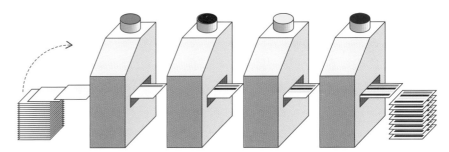

Sheet-fed presses come in many different sizes:
- 36 × 52 cm (14 × 20½ in) and 52 × 72 cm (20½ × 28½ in) formats are used for small 'commercial' products: business cards, small brochures with four, eight or sixteen pages on a short print run and anything similar to a postcard, a small poster or a flyer.
- 70 × 100 cm (27½ × 39¼ in), 72 × 102 cm (28½ × 40 in) and 75 × 106 cm (29½ × 41¾ in) formats are the most common and cover both the commercial market and publishing of coffee table books, magazines and luxury brochures as well as road atlases and gift wrap. Standard size 64 × 88 cm (25 × 34½ in) and 70 × 100 cm (27½ × 39¼ in) paper can also be used for these purposes.
- Medium 98 × 130 cm (38½ × 51 in) and 100 × 140 cm (39¼ × 55 in) formats are widely used for packaging.
- 120 × 160 cm (47¼ × 63 in) and 130 × 185 cm (51 × 73 in) formats, known as XXL, can be used for printing newspapers and school textbooks, comic and illustrated books in general. These machines perform similarly to small web presses, and even rival them on print runs of less than 15,000 to 20,000 copies. For large-format machines, the paper is produced by calculating its size as accurately as possible in relation to the printed surface. Unlike web presses, the height and width of the sheet are both variables and may be smaller than the print form, i.e., the plate (see page 123).

How do you get from an RGB file to a sheet printed in CMYK?

The start point is the purely digital line screen on a monitor in the RGB workspace; this is then converted into the CMYK four-colour space to reconstitute a line screen made of palpable analogue elements, i.e., lines of ink dots on a plate. These dots are then transferred to a sheet using the offset double transfer system. So, the screen pixels will have been converted into printable dots to make a halftone screen that is measured in lines per inch (LPI). The more coating a paper stock has, the more it can support a high (fine) line screen (dots closer together); on uncoated paper, ink penetrates the fibres more easily, the ink dots are more sensitive to pressure during transfer and therefore dot gain is more likely to occur. This is why a loose, coarser line screen with dots further apart is used for papers that 'drink' more. 133 LPI is generally used for uncoated paper; 150 LPI suffices for ordinary coated paper, but 175, 200 or even

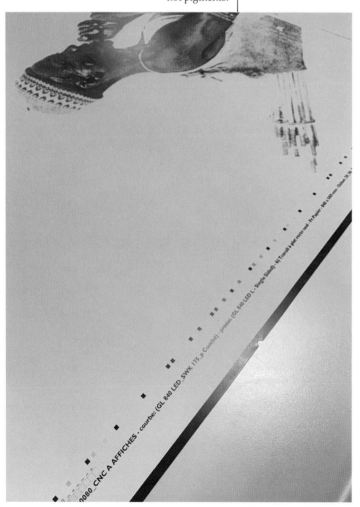

The plate prepared for printing: the black layer contains most of the details of an image. The blue colour has no connection to what will be printed; it is the emulsion left on the plate after exposure and is the 'vehicle' that picks up the ink from the inking roller and transfers it to the blanket for printing. All four plates are blue: they contain information, not pigments.

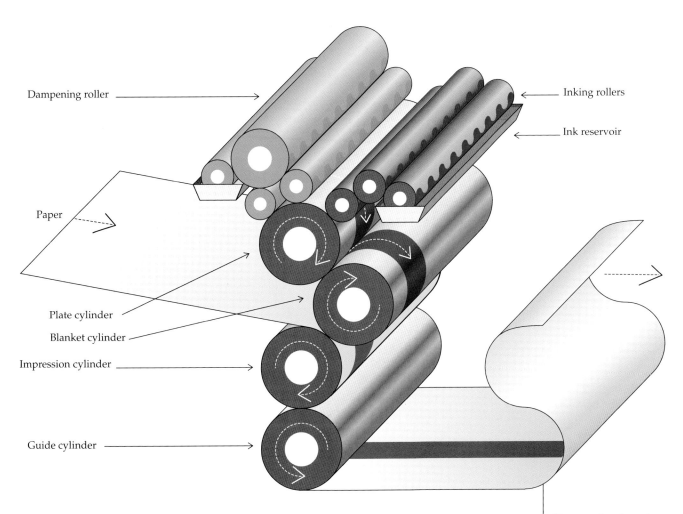

Dampening roller

Inking rollers

Ink reservoir

Paper

Plate cylinder

Blanket cylinder

Impression cylinder

Guide cylinder

These are the elements in a printing unit on an offset machine. You simply multiply by four for four-colour printing and so on, up to the number of colours available.

THE MECHANICS OF OFFSET PRINTING

Offset, in this case, means transfer.

The offset process is based on a simple physical and chemical principle: water and oil naturally repel one another. Inking and dampening rollers send the oil-based ink, along with a water and alcohol solution, onto a plate affixed to a first cylinder. This plate consists of a lipophilic polymer layer that attracts fat, and a hydrophilic layer that attracts water and prevents the ink from being deposited on it. When the plate is engraved, the dots corresponding to our screen are burnt onto a polymer layer. The lines of separate dots are transferred from the plate to the blanket, which in turn applies the pressure required to transfer them to the sheet of paper. This is a double transfer.

The ink reservoirs on an offset press; here in an eight-colour machine, we can see two rows each of yellow, magenta, cyan and black.

220 LPI is used in sheet-fed offset for jobs requiring higher levels of colour quality and detail.

<u>Dot gain and dot loss</u>: this is a phenomenon that is now fairly well-managed, if not eliminated, on modern presses thanks to the dot accuracy achieved on the plates in prepress. We mention it here to illustrate how ink behaves on different types of paper. When you put jam between two slices of bread and you hold the sandwich in your hands, the jam oozes out if there is more of it than the bread can absorb. The ability to contain the jam varies depending on whether you are using sliced bread, toast or farmhouse bread with well-oxygenated dough. You'll probably apply more or less pressure according to the type of bread, and, of course, the quantity of jam will vary according to how sweet-toothed you are. You need to find the right ratio between the paper (the bread), the blanket (your hands) and the quantity of ink (the jam). This brings us to **the superposition rate** of the four layers of ink; in other words, the setting done in repro that enables the press operator to do their work correctly.

THE FUTURE OF OFFSET?

There are sheet-fed presses for 70 × 100 cm (27½ × 39¼ in) sheets called HUV. These are now being replaced by more energy-efficient LED systems that have an HUV/LED oven at the output to cure the ink so very high inking densities can be applied without set-off issues, i.e., specks of dirt caused by ink transfer from one page to the next when the ink is not correctly absorbed by the paper (see page 195). The inks thus captured on the surface of the paper produce very vivid colours with a broader palette than the traditional spectrum, including on uncoated paper. This averts porosity and colour fading problems after drying.

This system enables us to reduce the quantity of ink used, and avoid having to use protective varnishes that tend to flatten the final printed result. It is also possible to use silk-screen varnishes inline with the same precision as the offset dot to highlight very fine details. Speciality papers such as mirror, gold or silver can also be used in this kind of printing. Finally, a white backing with white ink can be used (something that is impossible in traditional offset), creating the necessary opacity for four-colour overprinting on kraft and coloured paper (see page 174), or on transparent plastic. This system is very good for accuracy, brightness and sheen that cannot be achieved elsewhere. It has all the advantages of web and sheet-fed presses with the added bonus of silk-screen printing, so what's not to like? The only downsides at the moment are that some brands are still struggling to match all Pantones, and that they are more expensive. There are also issues with chemical components in UV inks, causing some to be on safety watchlists.

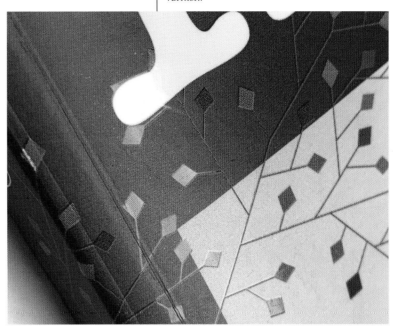

A selective offset varnish.

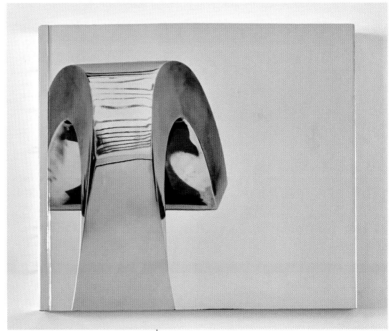

Print on mirror-effect paper.

Top: a proofer for printing digital
proofs in a repro studio.
Bottom: a digital press.

Digital printing

This works on the principle of an upgraded photocopier, to put it in very simple terms. **An image is reproduced instantaneously from a file, with no interruption from digital flows, no print form (no cylinder, no plates), by sublimation, electrostatic printing or inkjet transfer.**

Under the umbrella term 'digital printing' we find:

– Toner printing: laser printers where the image appears on the sheet through powder transfer.

– Inkjet with continuous drop (faster) or drop-on-demand (higher quality) or combined systems that can be modular based on what your priority is. These range from your A4- or A3-format office printer with four ink cartridges to top-of-the-range printers in prepresses, which print with six to twelve cartridges to reproduce as many hues as an offset press. They are specially calibrated and parameterized to reliably (i.e., according to contractual obligations) represent the colours that can be printed in offset. The same principle applies to large-format printers for producing tarpaulins, window stickers and other plotter proofs of varying formats for printing on all kinds of substrates: plastic, glass, Perspex and fabric.

– **Digital 'presses'*: these offer between one and five colours with the possibility of inline softcover binding, and can handle print runs of a few dozen to a few hundred copies.** Nowadays, there are some with almost identical quality to offset, which remains the benchmark. The format is limited to 53 × 75 cm (21 × 29½ in). They can print on the same grammages of paper as an offset press.

– Digital web presses: they offer between one and five colours, they are between 40 and 70 cm (15¾ × 27½ in) wide, and print on coated or uncoated papers from 70 to 140gsm. These machines have no plates, but in all other aspects they function the same as any other web press, with paper on reels that pass through folding cones and come out as folded signatures, which may even be bound in the process.

Between the time of writing and the time you read this, some of this information will probably have changed. Print runs in printing presses are falling, digital printing speeds are increasing, and digital is gradually eating into the offset market. It is striking to note that one person with a computer can now produce the same quantity that requires several people in prepress and offset printing.

*This term is widely used but not entirely correct here. On a digital printer there is no pressure or dampening as there is in offset, because printing is done with toners on sheet-fed machines and inkjet on web digital machines.

THE AWKWARD QUESTION

Why can't I print Pantone on a digital sheet-fed or digital web press?

A Pantone is a combination of oil-based inks specifically used in the offset system, whereas digital has its own powder-based toners and inks. Any Pantone colour in a file would inevitably be reinterpreted in four-colour and printed with the number of inks/toners used by each printing system: four, six or more. However, it has recently become possible to produce some fluorescent spot colours with HP-specific toners.

A digital web press.

WHAT ARE THE ADVANTAGES OF DIGITAL PRINTING?

On sheet-fed machines, sheets of paper are printed on both sides, assembled without folding or sewing and glued together as a block. This frees us from the constraints associated with assembling and finishing signatures in offset printing, and also allows random combinations of different papers in the same block. There are no plates or paper passes, which renders fixed costs almost non-existent. On digital web presses, the notions of imposition and signatures resurface – although there are no forms/plates – because the folding process is mechanical rather than digital. Digital web presses as a technology sit halfway between traditional and digital printing and are used for printing documents and books that would not otherwise exist (self-publishing, family publishing, theses and university publications, small catalogues and brochures, programmes, menus). They have changed the cost of printed materials, especially books, making it possible to republish out-of-print books and reprint very small quantities, bypassing the problems of tying up money, storage and potential deterioration of the items.

Print on demand, although not a technique in itself but more related to information technology, makes it possible to order a single copy or several units of printed material. This is already in use by legal and educational publishers. In the foreseeable future, we could envisage bookshops and press outlets printing single paper copies of novels, your daily newspaper or your favourite magazine while you wait, with the publisher holding onto the matrix. This obviously limits the choice of paper and finishes.

The hybrid nature of digital means it can be linked to databases and generate documents in which text and images can vary from one copy to another. This is very appealing for direct marketing, for example, for price lists, directories and any personalized publications.

Whatever happens, there will always be countless, unpredictable developments in the printing sector: the performance level of the LANDA S10 Nanographic Printing Press is already incredible. It is a 75 × 105 cm (29½ × 41¼ in) format digital press, with eight printing units: CMYK + orange/green/violet + spot colour; it prints four colours on both sides or eight colours inline at a rate of 6,500 to 13,000 sheets per hour. The press uses nanotechnology to print with powders so fine they could almost be liquid inks. At this level, talking about line screen no longer really has any meaning. At the other end of personalized digital printing, there are apps like Fizzer to send postcards from your smartphone from anywhere to anyone.

WHAT ARE THE DISADVANTAGES OF DIGITAL PRINTING?

The finishing options, often inline, are limited. Adding flaps to a cover or sewing signatures (a maximum of four pages) are rare and expensive operations.

From your office printer and photocopiers right up to sophisticated sheet-fed and web presses, these are all integrated systems that use proprietary inks. The high cost of these inks limits further development of the aforementioned techniques in digital printing. Then there are the characteristics of the inks themselves, which are not really recyclable.

Environmental management issues arise with toners that are either combined with solvents (HP) or silicon (KODAK) to fix them on the printed substrate. These powders are also soluble in water; although there are some so-called 'food-grade' inks for printing pizza boxes and other packaging, the environmental issues have not been properly addressed as is the case with offset printing.

Not all papers are suitable for all digital machines: many digital printers use a specific stock – designed for digital presses – that has been treated with a thin, transparent coating called 'lick coating'. This preparation, and the special ink required for digital printing, mean that it is more expensive than offset printing.

This explains why digital printing becomes less and less economical as the print run increases, when it becomes more economical to use an offset press. Speed and quality are other considerations when deciding on whether to use digital printing – digital presses are slower and the quality is not as good as offset.

See page 130 for a price comparison of digital and offset printing.

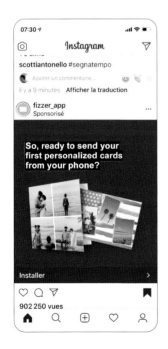

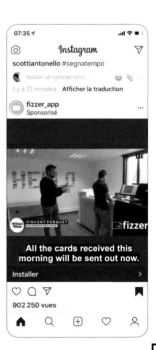

Glossy silk-screen
varnish on mass-
dyed uncoated card.

Silk-screen printing or serigraphy

From the Latin *sericum* (silk) and the Greek *graphein* (to write), this is a technique that was notably developed by the Japanese to print kimonos. Silk-screen printing **is the most widely used technique for reliable repetition of a pattern along with great rendering of beautiful, bright and saturated colours** on substrates ranging from textiles, metal, glass and acrylic to art paper and wood. In simple terms, it is a stencil technique, in which a negative image is transferred onto a screen held on a frame that transfers ink onto the object, before it is passed through a drying tunnel. Silk-screen printing is a very specialized craft: the printer has to be able to visualize the final result as the colours are usually printed one after the other with intermediary drying periods.

The main advantage of silk-screen printing is that it can print on large surfaces and be applied to objects that are not necessarily flat (bottles, boxes, textiles).

Another advantage is the ability to print colour on coloured substrates without colour shift. Offset inks are transparent and their colours combine with those of the underlying paper, while **screen printing inks have extensive coverage and remain entirely on the surface**. However, care needs to be taken with very dark fabrics and papers where the colours might show through if very light-coloured inks are used: to counteract this problem, an opaque white ink backing is applied to create opacity between the substrate and the printed colour.

Coated card printed with a Pantone. Dots of UV transparent relief varnish and a glossy black varnish have been added.

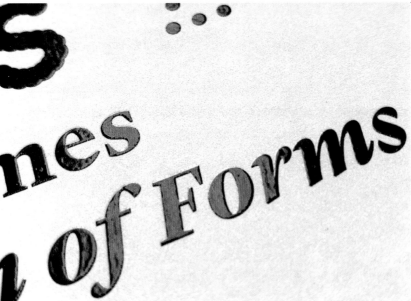

Black relief varnish on uncoated card.

We often use silk-screen printing for producing books and brochures when we want to decorate the covers with all kinds of finishes (spot, high-build varnish, glitter, mirror, grainy varnish). We will discuss this in the chapter on finishing.

Silk-screen printing is fairly expensive for more than two colours, and four-colour printing only pays for itself on a large print run because of the high fixed costs. If you need to print a lot of colours, it's best to use the **screen print transfer technique** that gives you complete freedom and also allows you to use the Pantone range on a white ink base. This technique is much more flexible than offset in terms of the surfaces you can print on, including textiles.

Left to right: a screen varnish that imitates cloth, silver matt spot varnish and red gloss spot varnish.

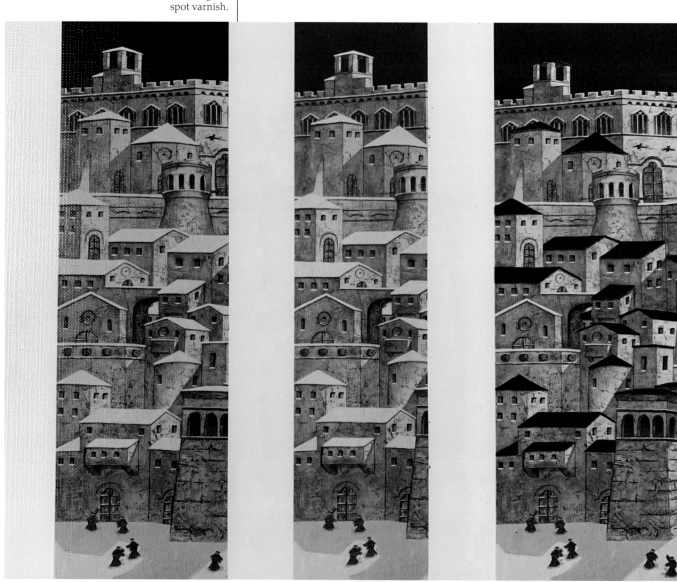

Other techniques

Embossing

Engraving a pattern on a metal tool that is pressed onto a given material to leave an imprint; a foil or a pastel can be added (we will discuss this in more detail in the chapter on finishing, see pages 236 to 242).

Laser marking

Laser can reproduce text and images with precision and without chemicals, by burning the surface of a material to a greater or lesser degree. The result is only monochrome or tone on tone, but is suitable for personalizing objects such as pens, key rings, memory sticks, or fleece clothing, if you're planning a textile component in your communication project.

Above, the plate used to print a silver foil on uncoated card previously printed in four-colour.

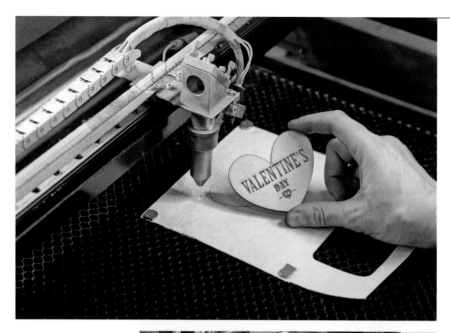

Laser marking technique.

Tampography (or pad printing)

This is the principle of the rubber stamp: the print form is a plate etched using a chemical process that transfers ink onto the artwork area. Four-colour processes and spot colours can be used.

This is a cheap, rapid and highly precise system that can only be used on small objects.

It is used to print bottle tops, keyboard keys, bottles, and household electronic goods components, i.e., any rigid or semi-rigid material produced in small or large series.

The inks are not long-lasting, especially on metal as it does not absorb them.

Flexography technique.

Ceramic transfer technique

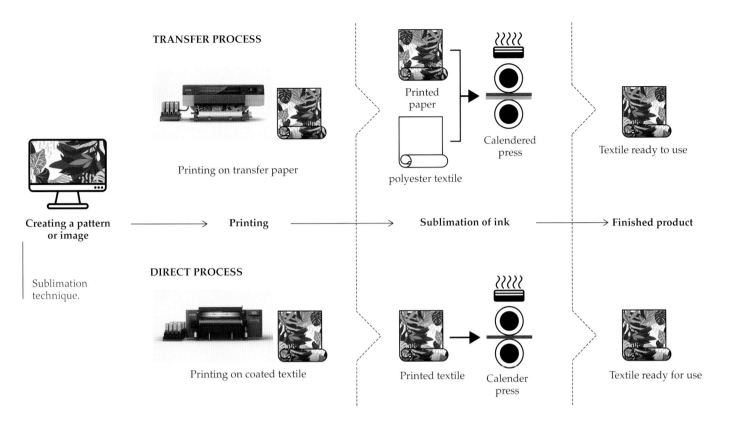

TRANSFER PROCESS

Printing on transfer paper

Printed paper

polyester textile

Calendered press

Textile ready to use

Creating a pattern or image

Sublimation technique.

Printing

Sublimation of ink

Finished product

DIRECT PROCESS

Printing on coated textile

Printed textile

Calender press

Textile ready for use

Flexography

Again, this works on the principle of the ink pad but on a larger scale: printing can be done on forms of up to 1.3 × 2 m (51 × 78¾ in).

Flexography can do four-colour printing on varied substrates and uses liquid inks (not the ones used in offset): water-based inks on corrugated cardboard, solvent-based inks on plastic bags made of polyethylene film and ultra-fast-drying UV inks.

Ceramic transfer

This is done through decalcomania (decorative transfer), and then fired so the image penetrates the material.

Sublimation

This is a digital technique that consists of printing an image on a transfer paper, then transferring it using a heat press to a substrate comprising at least 50% polyester. This method makes the print indelible and water-resistant.

Checklist
UNDERSTAND PRINTING TECHNIQUES

Quickly determine which printing system you are going to use to produce the printed object.

Check with your service provider the best way to prepare the files.

IV

CHOOSE

Having at least a basic mastery of the vocabulary is essential to understanding the connections between different aspects of graphics production. Here we look at a few common key words, so you'll be able to understand the terms used when you ask for quotes that involve technical data and strategic choices.

Being precise and thorough at every stage is useful, and it's the best way to gauge your ignorance of a subject and make rapid progress.

The more you work with your printer to specify what you want, the more you'll become aware of the challenges arising from details that may seem insignificant but that play a decisive part in the budget allocated to your project: reducing a format by 5 mm (¼ in) or sacrificing four pages on a block can save you a lot of money. Similarly, you'll realize that the more you increase the print run or pagination, the more offset printing outstrips digital for small publications with a limited number of copies.

Ask your partners about the subjects they specialize in and never make a final decision before you're sure you've asked all the questions.

Format and size

The terms 'format' and 'size' appear at several points during production. Let's start with document format. Here is a document consisting of four pages.

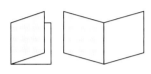

You are working on a 28 × 14 cm (11 × 5½ in) **open format** that, when folded in half, will result in a 14 × 14 cm (5½ × 5½ in) **closed format**. If it's not square, it's rectangular and there are two possible orientations:
– vertical = **portrait**, eg. 21 × 29.7 cm (8¼ × 11¾ in).
– horizontal = **landscape**, eg. 29.7 × 21 cm (11¾ × 8¼ in).

Vertical
= *portrait*

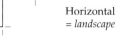

Horizontal
= *landscape*

DIVIDING INTO THE INFINITELY SMALL

Do you know why an A4 format is the size it is? If a square has 21 cm (8¼ in) sides, the diagonal would be 29.7 cm (11¾ in). A square metre, i.e., 84.1 × 118.9 cm (33 × 47 in), corresponds to the A0 format that can be divided in two as many times as you want while retaining the same proportions. So A0/2 = A1, A1/2 = A2, A2/2 = A3 and so on and so on. Each time, the long side is always equal to the diagonal of a square made from the short side.

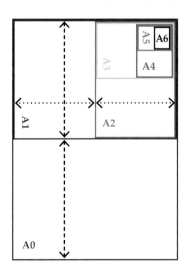

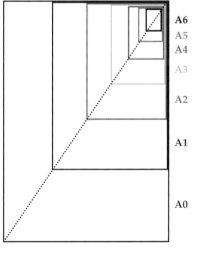

STANDARD US PAPER FORMATS	
Letter (ANSI A)	8.5 × 11"
Tabloid (ANSI B)	11 × 17"
Arch C	18 × 24"
Arch D	24 × 36"
Arch E	36 × 48"

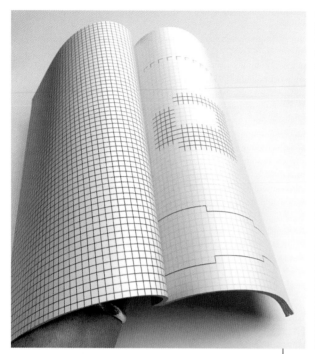

The flexibility of a low-grammage coated paper (left) versus the rigidity of a printed block on paper that is thick (high bulk matt art) and against the grain.

BANANA SKIN

In the fine arts world, the long side of a picture is always expressed first: P for Portrait (18 × 14 cm/7 × 5½ in), vertical rectangle; L for Landscape, horizontal (18 × 12 cm/7 × 4¾ in); M for Marine, panoramic (18 × 10 cm/ 7 × 4 in). If a museum or art gallery asks you for a 28 × 22 cm (11 × 8½ in) brochure, they are very probably asking for portrait format. But check with them if you're not sure!

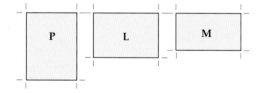

According to convention, we always indicate the base first. This simple detail indicates to a printer what type of format you want. If you write 29.7 × 21 cm (11¾ × 8¼ in), the estimator understands that you want a horizontal format: base 29.7 cm (11¾ in), height 21 cm (8¼ in). Don't be afraid of repeating yourself; if you're not sure, write it out in full: that reassures the estimator and avoids misunderstandings.

Indicating the format correctly is important for several reasons, not least of which is to enable the printer to calculate the sheet size (or reel width) that they need to order, taking the finishing into account. We have seen that paper is like fabric, an aggregate of fibres that are more elastic in one direction than the other. **The printer needs to order the paper so that the fibres are parallel to the spine when the sheets are printed, folded and assembled into a block** (see page 120). If you do not express this correctly, the paper stock may end up being ordered 'against the grain', which means the object might not open properly and cause a nasty curled edge (see page 67). The thicker the paper, the more rigid it is, making defects more visible.

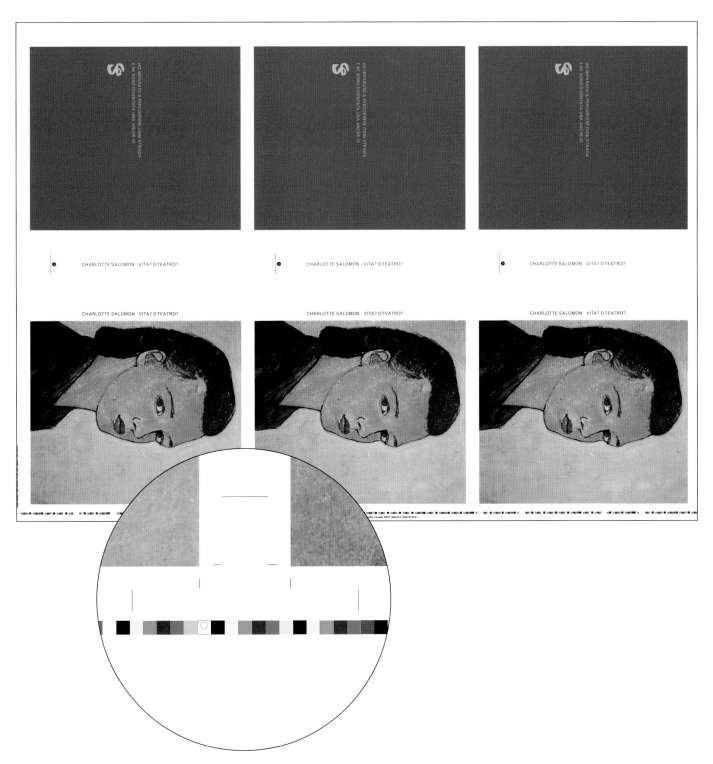

When you specify a size, it is always referred to as a trim size, i.e., the final format of an object after trimming. When printing greetings cards or a book cover, the printer will do an imposition, repeating the file a number of times on their sheet. They need to plan for spacing between the different duplicated elements to be able to do the finishing correctly.

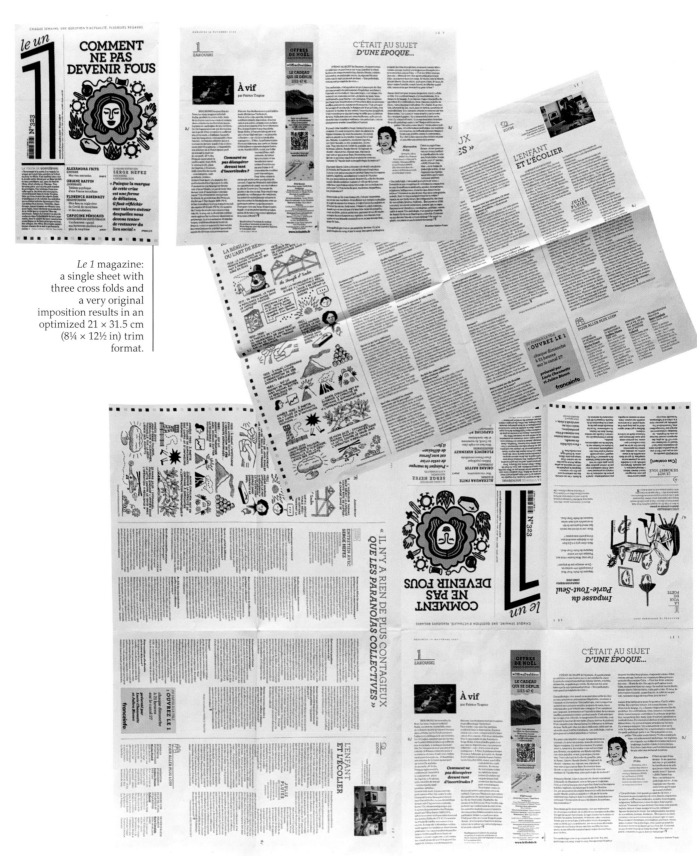

Le 1 magazine: a single sheet with three cross folds and a very original imposition results in an optimized 21 × 31.5 cm (8¼ × 12½ in) trim format.

BANANA SKIN

There is a second reason to always refer to the trim size: the size of the inner block and the cover are identical for a brochure; both are cut at the same time after the cover has been glued to the block (see pages 205 and 212).

However, for a hardcover book, the cover is larger than the inner block. If you're basing your request for a quote on a specific book, give the dimensions of the inner block and not the book with the cover closed.

The trim is where the guillotine cuts the paper (or other printed material). The bleed is the thin band of 3 to 5 mm of paper added to allow for any variation during the cutting process, which can be relatively inaccurate. Including the bleed ensures no unprinted paper shows at the margins.

To give an example, a 10.5 × 15 cm (4 × 6 in) postcard will actually occupy a space of 11 × 15.5 cm (4¼ × 6⅛ in) repeated x times on the sheet.

This helps us to understand why, when a document is laid out, 3 to 5 mm of any image intended to 'bleed off' the page (i.e. have no margins) should always overflow into the bleed.

The size of the printing machine also determines the size of the paper to be ordered based on the imposition of the pages on the sheet. We talk about this at greater length in the following pages and in the chapter on finishing.

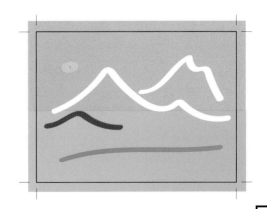

Why does a format that's only slightly bigger cost me a lot more?

Since **everything depends on a small equation between the size of the printed object, the size of the machine and the size of the paper,** you have to watch out for the tiniest variations that could tip you over into a bigger budget. Let's take the example of a 16-page brochure with a trim size of 22 × 28 cm (8½ × 11 in), printed on a small 70 × 100 machine with a standard 70 × 100 cm (27½ × 39¼ in) paper format. If you add a few millimetres to the height to give a final size of 22 × 29.7 cm (8½ × 11¾ in), it makes no difference because once the plate imposition with the trims and control bars has been arranged, the sheet is fully utilized.

However, if you want a height of 30.5 cm (12 in) for your brochure, these eight extra millimetres mean you have to change the imposition. You can only put twelve pages on the sheet, which has two disadvantages: the cost of an additional form for the four remaining pages and the paper wastage on the first form.

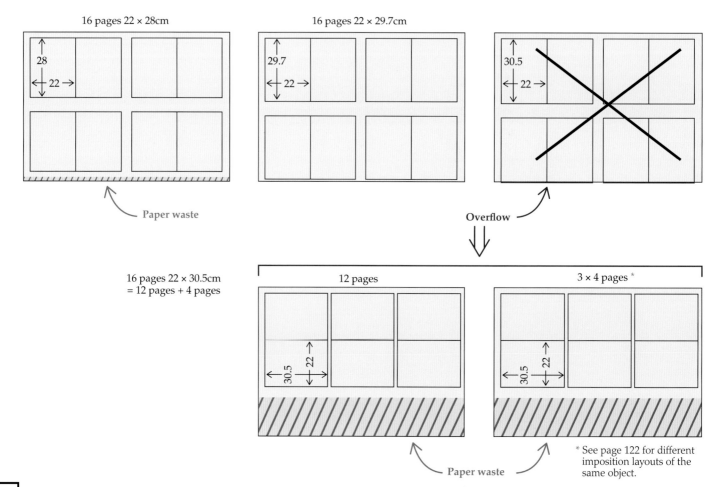

16 pages 22 × 28cm

28

22

Paper waste

16 pages 22 × 29.7cm

29.7

22

30.5

22

Overflow

16 pages 22 × 30.5cm
= 12 pages + 4 pages

12 pages

30.5　22

3 × 4 pages *

30.5　22

Paper waste

* See page 122 for different imposition layouts of the same object.

Pagination

What is a page, a sheet, a leaf, a signature...?

When you tear a **page** out of a magazine, do you really know what you're talking about?

What we call a page in everyday life is, in printing, a planar surface consisting of two sides, known in technical terms as recto and verso; in other words, two pages in the body of a printed work. These two pages together are known as **a leaf.** This is where finishing in its most basic form begins: to produce a flyer or a small poster, for example.

Note: A leaf is called a **panel** in the case of a leaflet.

A **sheet** is printed on a machine from the usable area of a **form** (or plate) and can be occupied in different ways:

a) fully by one single element: a large poster the same size as the form;

b) by a set of elements that are subsequently separated: 4 small posters, 16 postcards or 48 business cards;

c) by a defined number of consecutive pages in a signature, i.e., with the sheet folded once, twice or several times.

On a digital press, a series of leaves is printed with no pagination constraints, as the leaves are laid one on top of the other with no folding required: it is therefore possible to work in multiples of two.

On an offset press, as soon as we have a product consisting of a sequence

✳ TIP

If you have a six-page leaflet (three panels), consider removing 2 or 3 mm (around ⅛ in) from the outer edge of the inside panel to make it easier to fold. If you have a large roll fold leaflet, i.e., with several panels folded into each other, you need to remove an additional 2 mm on each panel. For an accordion fold, the problem doesn't arise because all the panels are identical.

ROLL FOLD

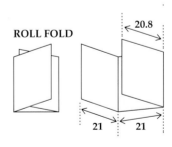

ACCORDION FOLD
Dimensions of closed format
= dimensions of all the panels

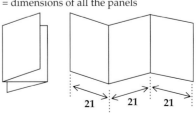

BANANA SKIN

Note, however, that it is possible to fold signatures of:
- 24 pages up to a grammage of 150gsm;
- 16 pages for a grammage of 170gsm;
- 8 pages maximum with 200gsm paper.

So stay vigilant and don't make a final decision before consulting your printer (see page 206).

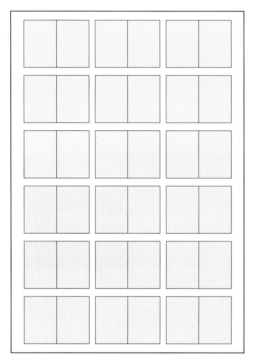

A sheet containing 48 pages

of different pages, **we get into the mechanics of imposition, i.e., laying out pages on a sheet, which are transformed into one or more signatures**. The latter are assembled to constitute a **block** that is either sewn, or ground and glued depending on the type of finishing and binding planned.

It is important to understand this essential part of the process so you can simultaneously plan for optimizing your pagination, for potentially alternating paper types and for adding inserts. Don't hesitate to ask your printer for the imposition, i.e., the number of pages per printed sheet and per folded signature. One, two or several signatures can be produced from one sheet.

How do I find the optimum number of pages (pagination – imposition)?

Once a sheet has been printed, it passes through a folding machine. Based on fairly complex imposition schemes that we won't go into here, this folds and transforms the sheet into either one or several signatures depending on sheet size and paper thickness.

When we print sheets or reels to generate signatures, two is a very inconvenient multiple, as it involves costly and complex assembly operations that are not always mechanically feasible.

A multiple of four pages is a minimum for easy mechanized folding and assembly operations. However, there is no magic formula that can be applied in all circumstances (especially when it comes to web presses), because the more pages there are in a signature, the more you optimize the cost of your product.

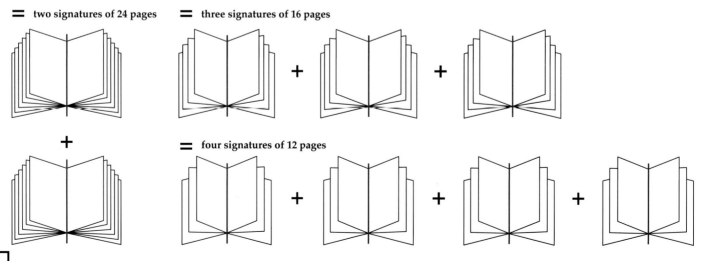

═ two signatures of 24 pages   ═ three signatures of 16 pages

═ four signatures of 12 pages

The secret of optimization in printing is to find the happy medium between the following:
– pagination,
– size of the trimmed block.
 But also…
– number of copies,
– size of the printing machine,
– paper grammage and type.
Don't worry: you don't have to learn all this like multiplication tables, and you certainly don't have to start solving quadratic equations: all parameters involved in printing and finishing – in addition to paper grammage, which can sometimes complicate matters – make your strategic choices too complex for you to tackle as a beginner. Briefly explaining them here is just a way to encourage you to consult your printer and benefit from their knowledge to be confident that you're doing the right thing.

A complete form that will make a 16-page signature: eight pages on one side (recto), eight pages on the other (verso).

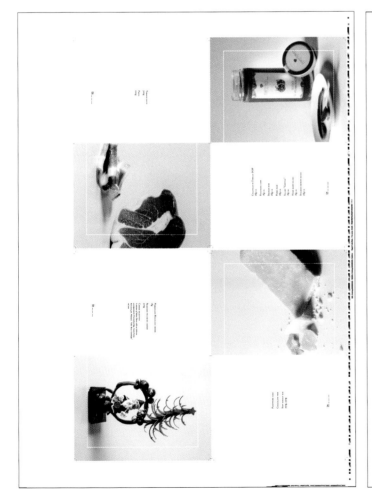

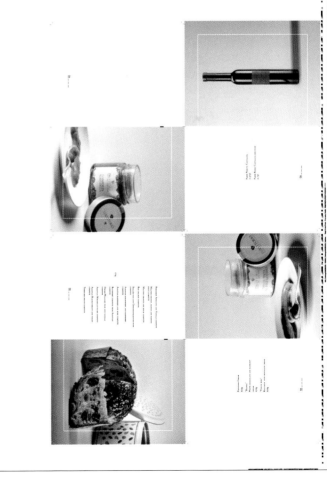

IMPOSITION FILE
PRINTING A 20-PAGE BOOKLET: 16 INTERIOR PAGES + 4 COVER PAGES

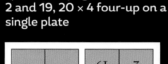

1 2 3 4 5 6 7 8 9 10 11 12 13 14 15 16 17 18 19 20

a) Interior: 16 pages numbered from 3 to 18, making 8 pages on both sides (recto/verso)

b) Cover: 4 pages numbered 1, 2 and 19, 20 × 4 four-up on a single plate

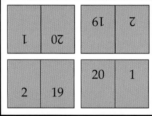

Plate 1, recto 8 p. × 2,000 copies

Plate 3, recto

+

+

Paper flipped on the verso and rotated 180°

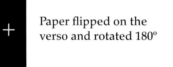

Plate 2, verso 8 p. × 2,000 copies

...and verso

=

=

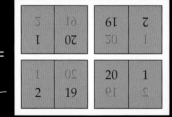

16 p recto/verso × 2,000 copies

4 × 4 pages × 500 copies = 2,000 covers

Graphic designers usually express pagination as shown in the diagram above, but printers separate the two interior and cover elements to make their plates.
It is best to get into the habit of supplying two files numbered 1 to 4 for the cover and 1 to 16 for the inside. This is essential when you have different stock for the cover, and absolutely vital for softcovers with flaps and hardcover books, where the cover is a different size from the inner block.

1	2	3	4
1	2	3	4
5	6	7	8
9	10	11	12
13	14	15	16

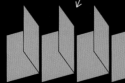

Whether you're printing on a web or a sheet-fed press, it's worth understanding the basic constraints:
– the number of pages per side of the sheet as specified in the printer's imposition,
– the number of pages planned per signature in the finishing phase.
The sheet-fed offset technique can help us understand the global mechanism of imposition.

For large-format presses (120 × 160 cm/47 × 63 in and above), the paper stock has to be produced to order in the correct format for your book; this is much cheaper because there won't be any wastage, but you should always plan for a slightly or considerably longer production time depending on the stock you are using. There are standard formats and therefore standard sheet sizes to fit the larger-format presses, and these are usually always in stock at the paper mill, for example crown quarto.

For small-format presses, the paper can be sourced quickly, because 64 × 88 cm (25 × 34½ in) and 70 × 100 cm (27½ × 39¼ in) formats are available in stock, but they are also more expensive. In addition, there is often some wastage because standard stock isn't necessarily suitable for your specific needs.

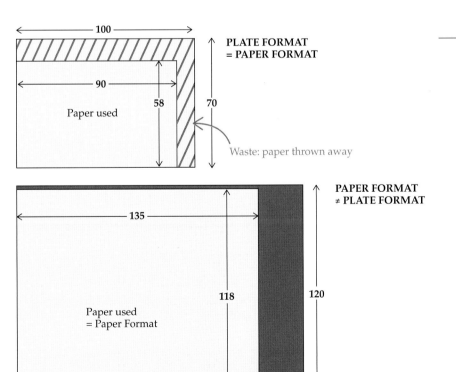

PLATE FORMAT
= PAPER FORMAT

Waste: paper thrown away

PAPER FORMAT
≠ PLATE FORMAT

Here is an example of a 48-page brochure in a 22 × 28 cm (8½ × 11 in) format.

a) three forms of 16 pages on a 70 × 100 machine with standard 70 × 100 paper (= six makereadies).

b) one form of 48 pages on a 120 × 160 machine with 135 × 118 paper made to order (two makereadies).

The choice you make will be dictated by your print run: if you can reach the minimum tonnage for production in an optimized format, you will end up with a single form (two makereadies). Otherwise, you will have to use standard size paper and print three forms (six makereadies).

THE CASE OF A 96-PAGE BROCHURE, 22 × 28 CM (8½ × 11 IN) CLOSED TRIMMED FORMAT

Possibility 1: you're planning a small or medium print run of 500 to 2,000 / 3,000 copies
1) 70 × 100 machine
Standard size paper
16 pages both sides per sheet

6 sheets – 12 makereadies

6 signatures of 16 pages

2) 100 × 140 machine
= standard size paper:
32 pages per sheet both sides
3 sheets – 6 makereadies
6 signatures of 16 pages

Possibility 2:
You're planning a larger print run, between 5,000 and 20,000 copies
3) 120 × 160 machine
paper size made to order
48 pages both sides
2 sheets – 4 makereadies
4 signatures of 24 pages
(if your paper is less than or equal to 150gsm)
or
6 signatures of 16 pages
(if your paper is over 150gsm)

We can immediately see the advantage of large-format printing when the print run permits, because we can reduce the number of plates and makereadies (and therefore the fixed costs) and pay for just the paper we need without the risk of wasting some of it by underusing standard size stock.

70 × 100 machine

Plate 1	Plate 2	Plate 3	Plate 4	Plate 5	Plate 6
Recto sig1 (16p.)	Verso sig1 (16p.)	Recto sig2 (16p.)	Verso sig2 (16p.)	Recto sig3 (16p.)	Verso sig3 (16p.)

Sheet 1   Sheet 2   Sheet 3

Plate 7	Plate 8	Plate 9	Plate 10	Plate 11	Plate 12
Recto sig4 (16p.)	Verso sig4 (16p.)	Recto sig5 (16p.)	Verso sig5 (16p.)	Recto sig6 (16p.)	Verso sig6 (16p.)

Sheet 4   Sheet 5   Sheet 6

100 × 140 machine

Plate 1	Plate 2	Plate 3	Plate 4	Plate 5	Plate 6
Recto sig1 (16p.)	Verso sig1 (16p.)	Recto sig3 (16p.)	Verso sig3 (16p.)	Recto sig5 (16p.)	Verso sig5 (16p.)
Recto sig2 (16p.)	Verso sig2 (16p.)	Recto sig4 (16p.)	Verso sig4 (16p.)	Recto sig6 (16p.)	Verso sig6 (16p.)

120 × 160 machine (paper <150g)

Plate 1	Plate 2	Plate 3	Plate 4
Recto sig1 (24p.)	Verso sig1 (24p.)	Recto sig3 (24p.)	Verso sig3 (24p.)
Recto sig2 (24p.)	Verso sig2 (24p.)	Recto sig4 (24p.)	Verso sig4 (24p.)

120 × 160 machine (paper >150g)

Plate 1	Plate 2	Plate 3	Plate 4
Recto sig1 (16p.) Recto sig2 (16p.) Recto sig3 (16p.)	Verso sig1 (16p.) Verso sig2 (16p.) Verso sig3 (16p.)	Recto sig4 (16p.) Recto sig5 (16p.) Recto sig6 (16p.)	Verso sig4 (16p.) Verso sig5 (16p.) Verso sig6 (16p.)

TOO MANY PAGES OR NOT ENOUGH?

Whereas in digital printing, multiples of two suffice for any kind of pagination, in offset it's best to work with more substantial modules.

For example:
Let's take our 96-page brochure printed in 2,000 copies on a 100 × 140 machine, which gives us three 32-page sheets for printing and six 16-page signatures for finishing.

A) You realize you have overestimated the pagination and you have four blank pages left; you have made no savings, because the third sheet will contain the space for the four unprinted pages, which will be cut and discarded.

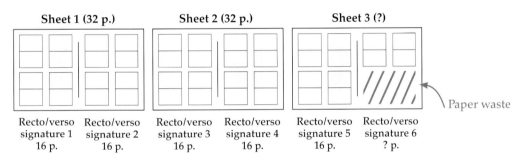

Sheet 1 (32 p.)	Sheet 2 (32 p.)	Sheet 3 (?)

Paper waste

Recto/verso signature 1 16 p.	Recto/verso signature 2 16 p.	Recto/verso signature 3 16 p.	Recto/verso signature 4 16 p.	Recto/verso signature 5 16 p.	Recto/verso signature 6 ? p.

B) You realize you have underestimated the pagination and you need four more pages; as your pagination was optimized for 96 pages, you will now have to plan a new print form and therefore new makereadies, not to mention cutting the sheet into four signatures of four pages. Is it worth it? Your printer will probably advise you to add eight pages in four-up on the 32-page print form, reducing the print run of the sheet to 500 copies; or, better still, add 16 pages two-up with a run of 1,000 copies.

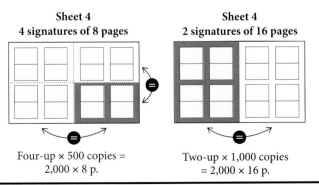

Sheet 4 4 signatures of 8 pages	Sheet 4 2 signatures of 16 pages
Four-up × 500 copies = 2,000 × 8 p.	Two-up × 1,000 copies = 2,000 × 16 p.

THE AWKWARD QUESTION

Why can't I print a 50-page brochure?

You can in digital printing, because a series of leaves are bound, but in offset, this causes a finishing problem, because you have to think in terms of signatures folded from a print form. Anything that goes through a finishing line should preferably be a multiple of four (see chapter on finishing, page 204).

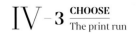
OPTIMIZATION MODULES: MAXIMUM BLOCK SIZE AND NUMBER OF RECTO/VERSO PAGES ACCORDING TO MACHINE SIZE

PORTRAIT BLOCK FORMAT

Machine	NUMBER OF PAGES PRINTED BOTH SIDES PER SHEET									
	128	96	80	72	64	48	40	32	16	8
120 × 160	14.2 × 19	19 × 19	15.5 × 28.5	19 × 25.6	19.5 × 28.5	26 × 28.5	29 × 31	29 × 38	-	-
100 × 140	11.7 × 16.5	15.8 × 16.5	17 × 18.6	15.8 × 22.3	17 × 23.5	22.8 × 23.5	24 × 27	24 × 34	35 × 49	-
70 × 100	-	-	-	-	-	16 × 16	16.5 × 19	16.5 × 24	24.5 × 33	34 × 49

LANDSCAPE BLOCK FORMAT

Machine	NUMBER OF RECTO/VERSO PAGES PER SHEET									
	128	96	80	72	64	48	40	32	16	8
120 × 160	19.5 × 13.7	19 × 19	29 × 15	26 × 18.6	29 × 19	29 × 25.6	29 × 29	38.5 × 28.5	-	-
100 × 140	17 × 11.2	17 × 15.3	24 × 13	22.8 × 15.3	24 × 16.5	24 × 22.3	-	34.5 × 23	48 × 34.5	-
70 × 100	-	-	-	-	16.5 × 12	16 × 16	-	24.5 × 16	33.5 × 24	48 × 34.5

This table shows the maximum trimmed size modules optimized for a particular pagination and a particular machine size.

The print run

Prices vary according to two parameters:
- **The fixed costs of the various makeready stages: these are costs that do not change** and that the printer will have to recoup, regardless of the print run;
- prepress operations (ripping your files, producing a control proof, making corrections to the control proof);
- the time it takes to set up the machine for each print form to calibrate density, pressure and registration;
- using some of the paper as pure loss to do the settings for colour calibrations and for the various finishing steps;
- depreciation and general costs (machines, premises, staff)

Starting up any machine has a minimum cost that will be spread over a given print run; the bigger this is, the more the cost will be diluted.

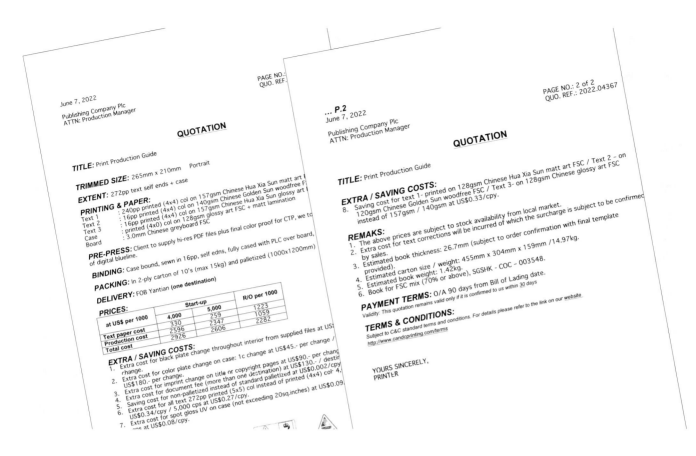

These costs are higher or lower depending on the type of printing: practically nothing for digital, significant for offset – especially if it is web printing – and very expensive for rotogravure.

– **Variable running costs**: these comprise only consumption linked to the print run, i.e., ink, paper and the hourly cost of the machines.

The more copies you print, the higher your total costs are, and the less your unit cost is. This helps you set up an operating account if you need to determine a sales price, per unit obviously, for your magazine, book or catalogue.

Your printer's quote can be expressed either as a unit price or as a global price for a given print run.

The quote often provides another amount: the run-on copy (or depending on standard practice, the next 100 or the next 1,000 copies): this is the price of any additional copies after your initial print run, which no longer includes the amortization of fixed costs for the initial set-up of all the machines involved.

If you order business cards, invitations, flyers or small brochures from a printer in town, it is highly likely you will receive the exact number of

CALCULATING THE COST OF A LARGER PRINT RUN

We have a quote that says:

For 2,000 copies, unit price €4.20 excl. VAT

Run-on copy: €3.60 excl. VAT

Theoretically, to calculate a larger print run, you would add as many run-ons as required:

2,000 copies   × €4.20 = €8,400

100 next copies   × €3.60 = €360

_____

2,100 copies   = €8,760

or €4.17 per copy

Here is the correct method for recalculating the price by extrapolating the fixed and variable costs:

€4.20 (fixed + variable) - €3.60 (variable) = €0.60

2,000 copies × 0.60 = €1,200: This is the total fixed cost.

To calculate the price of another print run, divide your fixed costs by the new print run and add the result to your variable costs.

A) To add 100 copies to your initial run:

Total fixed costs €1,200 / 2,100 copies = €0.57 (fixed costs) + €3.60 (variable costs) = €4.17

New unit price: €4.17

New total for 2,100 copies: €8,694

B) To subtract 100 copies from your initial run:

Total fixed costs €1,200 / 1,900 copies = €0.63 (fixed costs) + €3.60 (variable costs) = €4.23

New unit price: €4.23

New total for 1,900 copies: €8,037

These are theoretical calculations and suitable for very small changes in the print run. In reality, things are a bit more complicated because other parameters come into play, such as shipping costs, which depend on the number of copies per box and the number of boxes per pallet and finally the number of pallets loaded onto a truck. And one more box means one more pallet in the truck, which changes the total shipping cost.

copies ordered. What you don't know is that your printer has probably printed (and thrown away) a few more to protect themself against a shortfall in the print run that you might then complain about. You would be within your rights to ask them to reprint the missing copies, which would be disastrous for the printer, who would have to set up all the machines again for a derisory quantity of missing items.

Do you have to accept (and pay for) a higher or lower quantity than the print run you ordered?

The price of the run-on or of the 100 or 1,000 next copies is given for one simple reason: invoicing copies over and above the print run you have ordered.

A printing press and a finishing line are not bus routes with defined and predictable stops. To start a printing press, a few sheets are used to make the usual calibrations, and then a few more sheets are wasted to calibrate

BANANA SKIN

Depending on which country you are in, quotes may or may not include VAT or sales tax. If you print outside of the country to which you are delivering the books, you also need to take customs duties into account.

DIGITAL OR OFFSET?

You're working on a project for which the parameters have not yet been determined, and you're wondering which printing system will save you the most money. You start by asking a digital printer for quotes, then you ask for an offset quote. There you discover the advantages (sewn block) and the disadvantages (higher minimum print run, imposition required).

Here we have all the elements we need to consider our financial strategy:
If you have a limited budget, you take no risks and go for a small digital print run that doesn't tie up any money, and allows you to set some aside for however many reprints you need if your project is successful. Digital is perfect for this: it's a lot more expensive in variable costs, but enables you to complete a project with a lower initial investment, and without tying up money unnecessarily.
While it is cheaper to print long runs, increasing storage costs mean that many customers will choose to print shorter runs and more frequently. Once the fixed costs have been amortized, the variable costs are noticeably lower and your profit margin over the long term will be greater. So watch out for the point at which one technology becomes better than the other.

	DIGITAL	OFFSET
Print run	300 copies	500 copies
Closed format	16.5 × 24 cm (6½ × 9½ in)	Idem
	160 pages 4/4	160 pages: 5 × 32 pages, or 10 signatures of 16 pages
Paper	Matt coated 150 gsm	Idem
Cover	4 colours recto	Idem
Paper	Card coated one side 300gsm	Idem
Finishing	Perfect binding	Stitched signatures
Packaging	Shrink-wrapped	Idem
Shipping	An address in Lyon	Idem

300 copies	160 pages	€2,730			
	The next 100	€ 711			
500 copies	711 × 2 + 2,730	€4,152	**500 copies**	160 pages	€3,670
				The next 100	€183

the folding machine, a few more for the folded signatures and whole blocks to set the finishing line, and so on up to the final packaging. To give an example, a web offset press prints an average of 50,000 copies an hour and it's difficult to stop at the exact quantity required.

This cannot work any other way. Each machine in the production line needs to use and therefore consume a given quantity of paper to start and correctly set up production of sheets, signatures and blocks.

In short, a printer has to plan for unforeseen events over which they have varying degrees of control. **A basic rule of production is that you need to plan for a higher or lower degree of tolerance in the quantities delivered compared to the quantities ordered.** There is a documented scale of tolerance approved by European professional federations. As a general rule, the smaller the print run, the greater the tolerance. It comprises between 2 and 5% more or less than the initial order, depending on the specific case.

How to choose a printing system

You choose which type of printing system you want to use based on a combination of several technical factors: print run, pagination, finishing, paper grammage, etc. Sometimes the solution is self-evident; sometimes it depends on choices related to budget or product quality. Don't panic: we'll try to simplify it.

– If you have a few dozen brochures or a few hundred leaflets to produce, digital printing is the obvious choice, although with some size restrictions (A3+). A large poster cannot be done this way, for example.

– If you need to print a hundred copies of a thousand-page directory, you will print on low grammage stock on a digital press.

– If yours is a better-quality product, printed on beautiful paper of a certain thickness, you will have to choose between digital and offset presses. The print run is the determining factor as to whether you go for one or the other (see the example opposite).

– Once you've gone for offset, you can either print on a small machine with standard size stock or on a large machine when the print run, pagination and deadlines allow you to have the paper made to the optimal size. In this case, you make considerable savings on the makereadies (fewer plates) and finishing (fewer signatures).

– If you have a four-figure print run and several dozen pages on paper between 90 and 150gsm, you have to print on a sheet-fed or web offset press.

Checklist
CHOOSE

Determine which kind of printing is suitable for your document.

If you are printing in offset, ask the printer for their imposition (number of pages per print form and number of pages per finished signature).

Find out the delivery times for the paper stock you want. (You will only need to do this if you are ordering paper separately or asking your printer to order in a non-standard paper. If using standard paper, your printer would normally build paper delivery lead-times into the schedule they give you.)

Research the best pagination, and optimize the product in consultation with your printer.

Draw up the request for a quote, specifying the essential items; define the variables (in pagination or finishing); define the options that could be added to the chosen version.

Check the quote against your operating account; amend or change it if required before placing the order.

When should I request a new quote?

It is highly recommended that you ask for a new quote whenever anything is changed, and especially for a second print run if there is a numerical difference of more than a few hundred copies and any other major variation on the initial print run.

If you are undecided, it's best to get costings for several print runs from the outset, for the reasons explained on page 128.

V

COORDINATE

The worst might never happen, but anticipating it calmly is the best way to protect yourself against nasty surprises by minimizing their potential impact. As the philosopher Paul Ricœur said, a good production manager practises tragic optimism. You are, of course, very methodical so you'll have done what it takes to avoid any unfortunate mishaps, and you'll be justifiably proud of yourself when you find you've also prepared for an anomaly that no-one could have foreseen.

We can't repeat this enough: anticipate, make sure all communication is clear and simple, regularly reiterate instructions, stick to agreed delivery dates and to everything else you've agreed with your various partners. That's all it takes to ensure your production project turns out well. So here are the key stages.

The first is being aware of the challenges of colour management during the repro phase. The second is understanding prepress, i.e., correctly preparing the files to be printed. The third consists of monitoring all the other operations that manufacturers and others involved in the process are handling, but which are down to you to prepare well and closely monitor to ensure the successful outcome of your project.

Repro

These days, almost everyone thinks they can do the repro work themselves, and some people do it passably well. The tools for page layout and colour management are within everyone's reach, and technical progress has also enabled printers to work more or less without control proofs, from files that have been intelligently organized upstream.

It's all a question of what your requirements are in terms of quality, precision, technical complexity, and contractual demands. It's up to you where you set the bar, which responsibilities you are able to take on, and what your own technical skills allow you to do without outside help.

Professional photographers have a good understanding of RGB and know how to work with images in this particular workspace; graphic designers with a solid artistic and technical background know how to create wonderfully complex images using Illustrator, and resourceful project managers, editors and designers are often capable of handling a wide range of IT tools to produce multimedia communications on a wide variety of print substrates.

Depending on your role within the project and the end goal of your publication, you might find it useful to look carefully at the quality, price, delivery time, proximity and service criteria covered on pages 25–27. You'll see whether you can be confident in your own skills or those of your graphic designers, or if it's in your best interests to entrust all or part of a job to a colour management expert. **A prepress professional is neither a creative nor an IT expert but comes from a great tradition of craftsmanship and is a kind of bridge between a number of trades from the past and present. They have the technical knowledge, experience and sensitivity to understand what's at stake for you and to resolve your specific problems.**

Sometimes you can end up with a disappointing result from the printing press when you compare it to the proofs you had approved at the repro stage. However, **you will never get a good print from mediocre repro work**. Repro is sometimes the least important item in the budget and it would be a shame to exclude it. It can end up being a determining factor in the success of your project. In any case, you won't regret allocating a budget to this if it gives you extra peace of mind and better quality.

The inconsistencies of
acquisition…

… and of reproduction.

What is colour management?

Whether it's done by you, your graphic designer or your repro service, sooner or later you have to address the issue of colour management and ensure you have **everything in place for the images and colours to be reproduced as faithfully as possible**, whatever machine, inks and paper stock you're using.

Good colour management takes into account the input devices (scanner, camera), the output devices (monitor, printer, printing press) and finally the substrate you are printing on, which will have its own particular characteristics. **When you work with profiles, you adopt a protocol for moving from one machine to another and one colour space to another**, a protocol that permits everybody involved – graphic designers, repro and printers – to work with consistent parameters to maintain maximum coherence from the initial image file to the printed output.

The following issue first arises when the image is **acquired**, but it really stares you in the face when the image is **reproduced.**

Open a search engine and type in 'Mona Lisa/images'. Which one is true to the original and how can you reproduce it?

The issue here is twofold:

1– **Fidelity.** You can remain true to a document such as a watercolour or a photo print because you'll always have it in front of you as a basis for comparison to check the authenticity of the reproduction. With a digital image, the arbitrary nature of shooting conditions is the norm, so it's up to the person who commissions the work to define their truth and communicate precisely the criteria to follow for optimal reproduction of a source file. Fidelity is a subjective criterion.

2– **Consistency.** Whether you stay true to a given document or whether you make a personal interpretation for aesthetic or commercial reasons, you must make a decision so that your vision, your interpretation – in short, your subjective truth concerning a particular image – is scrupulously respected by whichever printer is responsible for reproducing it. Consistency is a universal criterion.

The repro specialist is first and foremost the guarantor of the correct reproduction of a visual element through their methods, which guarantee its reproducibility under all circumstances.

They work on calibrated screens and devices to ensure that their working environment remains consistent and conforms with international standards that ensure the same colours can be found elsewhere on similar equipment.

It's a bit like the principle behind a Big Mac, where you expect the same taste and texture at a McDonald's in Berlin, Beijing or Mexico City.

In the repro studio, basic adjustments are made to your image files and parameters are set so the images can be reproduced as faithfully as possible by the printer who subsequently works on them. That should be the case wherever the location (if you change printers) and whenever it is reproduced (if you reprint with the same file and the same paper).

Whatever the source material (opaque or transparent film, digital documents) and the target material (coated or uncoated paper, tarpaulin, fabric, acrylic), you need to be sure that the printed result is the one you are looking for. The repro specialist has the sensitivity to understand your needs and the expertise to translate the document that you provide, as well as your personal perception, into reliable and reproducible technical data.

They take all these parameters into account and ask the right questions to be able to proceed in the right way, i.e., with **standardized parameters**. They are neither medium nor magician, but experts whose business is to advise you. They cannot always guess what the client wants, but it is their job to understand you and clarify the points that are unclear. Discussing the issue in clear and simple terms is the best way to start. Once again, if you have any doubts, tell them: **simple, explicit, slightly repetitive communication is the secret ingredient for great production managers!**

THE TRUTH IS NOT THE SAME FOR EVERYONE

You can ask an operator to create a 'beautiful image' or to stay faithful to a particular work or product. They can do both, but don't expect them to automatically understand your wishes and needs, because they might be processing an image file of the Mona Lisa several times a week; on Monday for the Louvre Museum, who invite them to go and see the painting and reproduce it as faithfully as possible, on Wednesday for a cosmetics advertiser, who indulges in a little artifice to cover up the cracks in the painting to emphasize the smoothness of Mona Lisa's skin, on Friday for the leaflet of an underfunded charity that has lifted a medium-resolution image of the painting from the internet and will be content with an approximate reproduction to support a point it wants to make.

How to work with a repro professional

Some graphic designers have the skills to successfully perform all the repro tasks; if in doubt, it's best to entrust these tasks to an operator who has mastered all the nuances of page layout software. Such a person is essentially a graphic designer with technical skills over and above the artistic skills you would expect of someone in the creative industry.

What does a repro professional actually do?

When they are fully in charge of a project, a repro professional **converts digital images from RGB to CMYK**, calibrates **the superposition rate of the four colours** for printing on a given substrate and applies the appropriate ICC profile; if required, they work on **colour** and do some **retouching.** They show you the **contract proofs** that reflect the accuracy and printability of the colours. They check the various elements are **correctly assembled** in the page layout, prepare the **PDF files** for the printer and back up and store your archives.

This is how to proceed when you submit the initial documents to repro:
– Draw up a purchase order based on the terms in the quote and on the schedule; specify the total number of pages of your work and the number of documents to be processed, giving the necessary details (digital files to convert, opaque or transparent documents to scan). Be careful to allow time for the scans as it is a fairly lengthy process and not everyone in a studio is qualified to do it.
– It is essential to indicate the paper stock on which you're going to print (matt or gloss coated, white or coloured uncoated).
– Give a reference for the documents to be scanned. Accurately name the digital files. Never change the name of a file halfway through the process, otherwise it will not update correctly.
– Once you have completed your work, you need to collate the information in InDesign to check you haven't forgotten anything: images, fonts, crop marks, bleeds, transparencies.
– Give clear instructions on how you want the images to be processed.

Upon receipt of your materials, the repro service will:
- check the number of documents and files received against the order;
- check the resolution and reproduction formats required;
- save the images on a server (preferably duplicated in a secure backup);
- acknowledge receipt, ask any questions that are not answered in your initial instructions;
- confirm the date for the first proof correction session.

The repro studio now launches production of the visuals:
- for analogue documents: scanning;
- for digital documents: converting the visuals into CMYK, resampling if necessary;
- for everything: applying the appropriate print substrate profile, setting the superposition rate (see page 98) of the four colours, image cut-outs, cleaning the visuals, colour adjustment and possible retouches.
- produce, submit and possibly correct calibrated proofs (preferably in their studio, under standardized 5500° K/9440° F lighting).

BANANA SKIN

The closer you are to the finish line, the more the job becomes urgent, but this is exactly when you shouldn't skip any checks. The biggest production blunders often result from a little slacking off at the last minute, which is precisely when you have to stay focused. Just because your PDF was perfect last night doesn't mean it is still perfect after you've gone back to your native file to change a comma. You (or your graphic designer, or your operator) might be so focused on a typo that you don't notice the typeface in the title has changed because the fonts have not been reset correctly. Whenever you touch your file, even for something minor, follow a strict procedure and make sure this procedure is always the same.

After approval of the final proofs, repro will:
− update the files;
− proceed with the checks;
− generate certified PDF files, page by page, with technical mark-up;
− print laser proofs from the PDFs;
− archive all the native and PDF files.

Creating a PDF file might seem simple. However, the final PDF file, which the printer uses to rip the file to create the plates, has technical specifications that you may not be familiar with.

It's best to avoid improvising and leave the job to a professional: the repro specialist. Sending a PDF to a printer guarantees that your graphic design won't change, but also protects the printer against any inadvertent errors you may have made. **Check your PDFs very carefully before submitting them**, and take extra care over last-minute corrections: these are often done on the fly and over the phone, and that's where danger lurks.

WHAT IS A PDF?

The PDF or Portable Document Format encapsulates and preserves all the information contained in the page: images plus profiles, text plus fonts, vector elements and the layout itself.

It is used to view or print a page without altering its constituent elements, regardless of the input and output software and devices used.

Strange things can sometimes happen when a PDF is being created (fonts not recognized and replaced automatically, knockout information not managed, layer inversion, etc.); these anomalies do not arise from the PDF itself, but from poorly executed upstream commands. As soon as the slightest change is made to your source file, it is essential to go through a full validation process again to create a new PDF, because once created, it is set in stone.

THE AWKWARD QUESTION

Can the scanner I bought in a supermarket do a professional job?

This is a huge question. Repro studios have machines equipped with powerful lights and can achieve very high precision. Quality shop-bought machines do exist, but it all depends on your operating knowledge, the type of document to be scanned and the end result required.

What tools does a repro professional work with?

– Scanners (in the past, mostly rotary, now mostly flatbed).
– Powerful workstations.
– Software:
– Illustrator or Affinity Designer for vector images.
– Photoshop or Affinity Photo for all other images.
– Be aware that a vector image isn't suitable for modification in Photoshop.
– InDesign (or QuarkXPress) for page layout, i.e., assembling all the elements such as text, logos and images.
– Inkjet printers for proofs, laser printers for printing out reading and control copies.

How do they work?

– They scan the transparent continuous tones (transparencies), opaque, flexible or rigid continuous tones (colour or black and white photos, drawings, paintings). If necessary, they descreen the scanned documents from printed (screened) documents.
– They check the vector (non-screened) images in Illustrator, such as drawings, logos or barcodes created with computer programs. They make sure they are printable, then incorporate them into the layout but don't usually alter them. Sometimes, there are many layers and traces, and it can be difficult to dive into these vector constructions without running the risk of distorting the original construction. This kind of complex intervention should generally be left to the actual image designer.
– They convert, profile, correct, retouch, and cut out low-quality digital images, which consist of pixels and therefore depend on a specific initial resolution either at the time of shooting or when scanned.
– They incorporate all the above-mentioned elements into the layout.

The working method

On the one hand you have the layout file with the text, titles and other graphic and typographic elements and on the other, the images. The latter must eventually be placed on image layers provided for this purpose. **How do graphic designers and repro professionals work together?**

There are two methods:

1 – The graphic designer processes the colour separation in no particular order, because they want to start the colour work while taking the time to refine their mock-up alongside it. They have a very powerful computer and are comfortable with high-definition processing, which in some specific cases they also want to play around with a bit more. In this case, they supply the images to be processed with clear indications of the reproduction formats; the colour specialist will submit an initial proposal with digital proofs in no particular order, followed by a possible second (or third) set for the corrected images. When the designer has approved all the colour work, they now have the high-definition (HD) images to import into their file and can create the PDFs themself.

NAME A FILE ONCE AND ONCE ONLY

A file name is the equivalent of an address you put on an envelope so a postal worker can deliver it to the addressee. If the postman only had the recipient's photo on the envelope, they would have to knock on every door in the area in an attempt to recognize the person. Hence the importance of this definitive 'address', which must correspond to the recipient's mailbox (the image block). This name must remain unchanged throughout all the operations, otherwise, when the image is updated, it will be in the wrong place in the mock-up. The name can be very simple:

'Title'_001, _002, _003, etc., or it can be a complex code such as for a catalogue of artists' works or commercial products. If you replace an image during the process, it must be given a new name, because it's replacing the old image but not its identity.

2 – The designer may prefer to work with imposition format pages by attaching a layout file that includes framing and format information for the images. In most cases, they provide their repro expert with HD image files and possibly images to scan. The repro expert will quickly return them to the designer as low-definition files, which are much smaller and easier to handle. This gives the designer time to finalize the mock-up while repro works on the colour. Once the layout file is finalized, the designer gives it to the repro service, who update it from the HD files stored on their server, and then create the PDFs. At this stage, the designer can still make text corrections or minor framing or sizing changes to the images.

Working with colour

One day, in the scanner room of a large prepress company in Asia, I saw a poster of a baby, reproduced twelve times with subtle differences in the colour rendering of its skin. It was a guide for operators to be able to accurately calibrate the same subject for countries with different cultures and visions.

The example shown opposite follows the same rationale. Imagine a colour sample chart of foundation makeup on a screen in an online cosmetics store, but also in a printed catalogue and in a point-of-purchase display for shop windows or interiors with very different lighting. The differences in terms of printable dots between one shade of cream foundation and another are sometimes infinitesimal. To appreciate and reproduce these very close shades of colour, you need to ensure coherent processing of the image files, so that they can be reproduced accurately and consistently. **Whatever you're aiming to achieve, it's important to be able to predict the exact result you'll get from printing, and that's what repro does.**

We can do a lot of things from an image by playing with the curves to change the initial colour of a document.

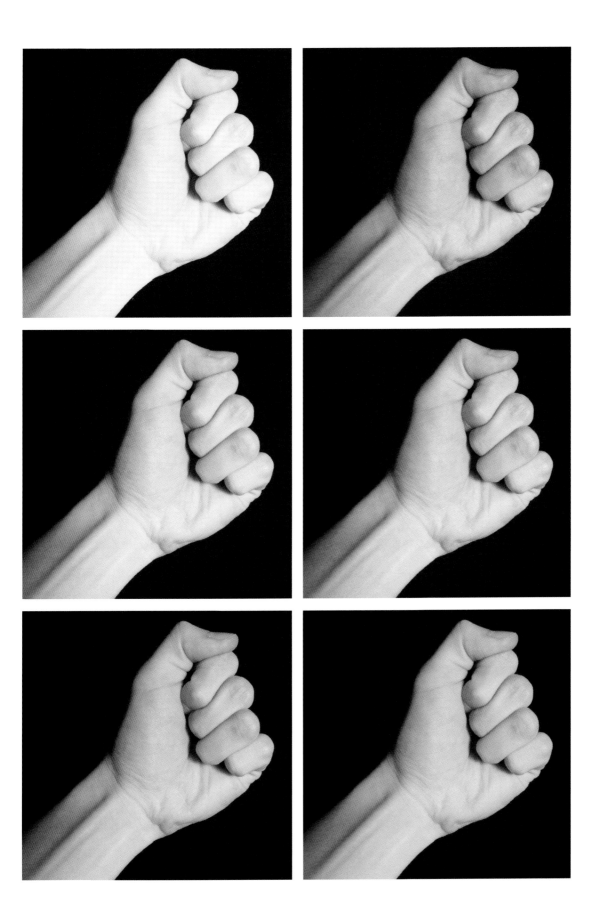

The advertising projects and graphic studies that Vasarely created between the late 1920s and mid-1940s offered a field of experimentation for forms that were to recur in later works. In *Mitin*, featuring a deformed checkerboard design accentuated by a classic shadowplay, we find a volume effect that was to run throughout Vasarely's work. As for the zebra pairs that feature in several works, like this 1932–1942 version, they announce future interplay based on the reversibility of positive and negative, through regular alternation of black and white stripes. Similarly, this study of movement representing concentric circles in water prefigures the wave radiation typical of Vasarely op art. It is therefore with figuration that the artist defined a basic repertoire and the plastic means that would lend the illusion of movement and volume to a two-dimensional surface.

9

Reinterpretation of an image (on the left) from an acquisition (on the right), along with a colour bar next to the photograph of the poster.

The start point and main priority for any good repro expert is remaining true to the document supplied. However, they receive disparate images with different constraints. So what do they do? In the case of artwork or transparencies, they scan the document while keeping a close eye on the original that they need to respect or reinterpret and that remains their reference throughout, even though you might either prefer to ignore it because it is damaged and poor quality or interpret it in a different way. (If that is what you want them to do, you should provide this kind of information before you have a document scanned.) In the past, we used to work from transparencies, which were developed with a colour gamut. The gamut was used to check the colour accuracy of the transparency and correct it if there was any suggestion that the film had suffered any colour distortions or had colour cast.

With digital, it's easy to rectify the defects of a bad acquisition.

In the case of a digital file from a photo shoot, the only reference is the file itself, which is viewed on a screen. The repro professional works with a **screen calibrated** to daylight (5500° K/9440° F), which allows them to view, modify, proof and print an image under consistent conditions, anywhere in the world.

They must be properly equipped with devices that are all calibrated in the same way to avoid blurriness and the randomness of the digital universe so that they can adhere to and apply objective standards and procedures as part of a **coherent workflow**. It's easy to understand why the first rule in the graphic production chain is to work under **standardized white light conditions**, i.e., the conditions you find at the printing press that enable the habitual calibrations to be done.

From left to right: the RAW file, the RGB file, the file converted into CMYK and the final version after colour work.

What type of image file should you work with?

A **RAW file** is a high-definition digital file (the equivalent of an analogue negative) that contains all the information about the shot; we see why there are millions of pixels in a 48-bit image (16 per RGB channel): **the density of information will therefore be almost comparable to the continuous tone of a camera film**. This file will be developed in a software programme such as Lightroom, or something similar, where it can be polished and deficiencies and defects in the shot remedied. This can also be done by the photographers themselves or in specialized laboratories.

An **RGB file** in a 16-bit Tiff format is good enough for ordinary images. **If you are offset printing, avoid providing JPEG files if you can**, as compression causes information loss, especially if the files are opened several

times. However, for very complex work such as creative retouching in the advertising industry, it is advisable to provide a RAW file so your service provider can get the best out of it.

At this point, the colour management expert can proceed in various ways: For a job with no particular difficulties on a homogenous set of illustrations (a single photographer, a single illustrator, composite so-called tint or halftone dots, or a standard level of quality in a heterogeneous set), the operator converts the RGB files into CMYK files, and does their settings: applying the appropriate ICC profile for the type of printing paper, setting the superposition rates (see page 98), colour calibration, cleaning and minor retouches, possible cut-out.

The advantage of working in a CMYK space is that the black layer is clearly visible, which is not the case in RGB. However, for a complex job

★ TIP
Some photo-processing software, such as Photoshop, permits the use of 'scripts' that automatically apply a series of settings for a specific batch of images rather than considering colour on a case-by-case basis.

Vibrant hues in a photo or original drawing are a challenge for repro

with all kinds of images and particularly bright colours or details in saturated hues (e.g., photos of the sea, children's books with fluorescent shades), the colour expert will prefer to work on RGB images, because Photoshop offers more options and tools in this space and there is a larger colour gamut to play with.

Sometimes, a combination of the two methods is used: the images are processed in detail in RGB, then converted into CMYK and re-worked in this space to fine-tune other aspects (contrasts and design).

For files that involve a lot of back and forth and colour work that will be queried, the repro service keeps a PSD file, i.e., the entire history of the work done on an image, with all the layers (or calques) rather than overwriting the different stages and keeping only the latest version.

The PSD format is essentially a way to save colour work, but it is not supported by printing devices. When you want to check the work that has been done and print a digital or laser proof, you need to export and convert this type of file into a format recognized by the printer's RIP:

– **TIFF** (a relatively large file) where you can always decide before doing the RIP if it's going to flatten the various layers or not;

– **EPS** and **JPEG** (small files), which, conversely, will automatically flatten the layers;

– **GIF** and **PNG**: formats suitable only for internet and smartphone applications.

BANANA SKIN

There is a .TIF variant for the .TIFF extension and a .JPG for the .JPEG extension. Be aware that they are not really interchangeable. If you modify a .TIFF and inadvertently save it with the .TIF extension, you are creating a new file, and this new identity could cause a problem when you update the file.

A CTP (*Computer to Plate*) machine that generates plates.

RIP

The RIP (Raster Image Processor) transforms data relative to colours known as continuous tones into halftone screens that can be printed. A printer has an internal RIP, whereas to print on a sheet-fed or web press, you have to go through the CTP (Computer to Plate) process in prepress; this transforms the data, attributes a screen to each colour layer, and produces a plate for each primary ink.

The same colour gamut produces different colours on uncoated, semi-matt and glossy proof paper.

Most Pantone colours cannot be reproduced on a digital proof.

Proofs and corrections

Digital proofs are created by prepress professionals using printers that have between eight and twelve cartridges: the four basic CMYK colours, their 'light' or 'pastel' versions, two or three Pantone colours and specific hues. **However, it is not possible to produce the full range of spot colours** and the machine's RIP instantly reinterprets them based on the number of colours that it can handle. These machines perform the difficult task of simulating offset printing conditions (i.e., a specific paper stock, water, oil-based inks and heat) with a different technology, similar to that of the photocopier, using different inks and paper stock. The internal software in digital plotters is designed to compensate for these differences.

Each type of printer is linked to the RIP management software: essentially GMG or EFFI.

The laser printers at repro studios use special paper (FUJI or generic) designed to correspond in terms of colour and reverberation to the specific nature of the toner, and aimed at replicating subsequent printing conditions. They simulate the surface of the main paper types (coated or uncoated, matt or glossy) and the ink absorption characteristics for each

BANANA SKIN

What is commonly referred to as matt paper at a repro studio is actually a paper that simulates uncoated, not matt coated paper. It's not your job to tell the repro professional which paper to use for their proofs; you just need to give them the key information they need to be able to apply the appropriate profile to the files and produce the proofs on the corresponding paper: the material on which the printer will work: paper (coated or uncoated, white or dyed); other materials such as metal, plastic, fabric or glass.

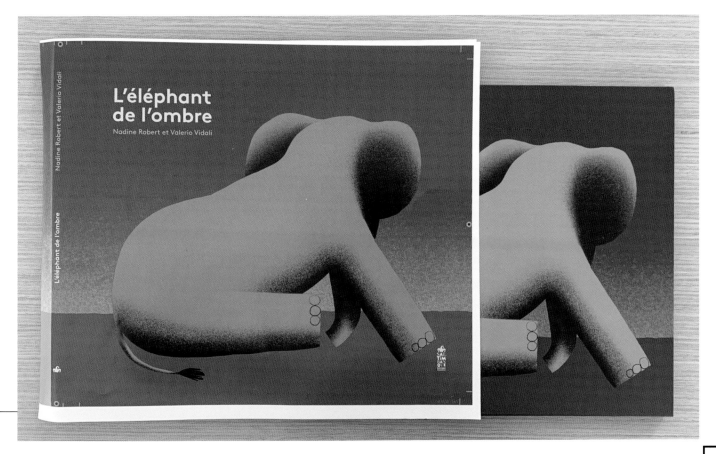

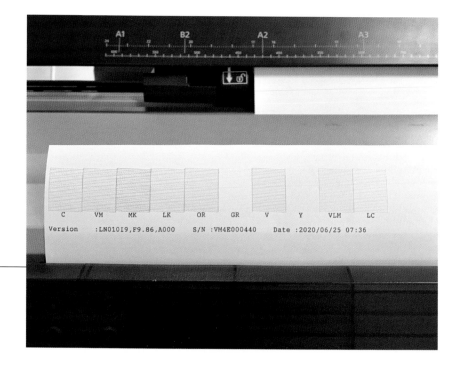

At the repro studio, the proofer that produces the digital proofs is regularly recalibrated to ensure parameters remain constant.

type of paper. **There are three major paper types for digital proofs: glossy, satin and matt.**

The control proofs produced by your repro service are printed by plotters on paper stock whose surface coating has been designed for the specific inks used in digital printing. These papers simulate the main types of 'real' printing paper and, above all, their capacity to absorb ink by reflecting light to a greater or lesser extent.

It should be noted that the growing demand for whiteness in recent years has been zealously adopted by paper manufacturers. The repro sector has had to adapt and the papers used for proofing have had to be modified to keep them consistent with the printing result. Optical Brightening Agent (OBA) papers now enable repro services to produce digital proofs with the latest-generation FOGRA standards to simulate the whiteness on the most recent ranges of printing stock.

The digital proofing process is subject to the same international standards and certifications that govern the entire graphic industry. Research is being done into the production of certified digital proofs from digital printers (Xerox, Minolta, Rocho, Canon-Konica). These proofs would be cheaper but for now they are unstable and, at the time of writing, certification is not yet possible.

BANANA SKIN

If you are providing a printer with images that have been worked on using a coated profile and proofs on digital paper (glossy or satin) so they can print on uncoated paper, you are in for a nasty surprise: coated paper can absorb much more ink than uncoated, and consequently your uncoated paper will receive excess density. The ink dots will spread and become too numerous on too many lines for a porous and absorbent paper: you lose finesse, highlights and detail.

An original and the corresponding scanned proof with colour adjustments.

How many corrections and new proofs can you request? The real question is: how much are you willing to pay to achieve your desired result? It's a tricky one…

When you are using digital images, the best way forward is to start by creating proofs of all your images. This gives you a document to work from. Obviously, this is a costly option. More often than not, you give instructions to the operator so they can adjust the colour to your liking before giving you 'reworked' proofs on which you can make some alterations before requesting the final control proofs.

If you have provided your repro expert with an original work, a photo print or a transparency, theoretically you can ask for as many corrections as you need to achieve a faithful reproduction, but we have seen that some colours are difficult to achieve on coated paper and downright impossible to reproduce on uncoated paper. Consequently, you'll need to compromise. While you have the right to push a colour expert to the limits of their talent, you should trust them if they tell you they can go no further. If your HDs are flawless and you're happy with them, you should expect a standard reproducible proof on paper stock simulating the one that will

✱ TIP
You can plan a meeting with your operator to review all the visuals on their screen so you can tell them what you want; then, you can mutually agree on a certain number of images representative of the whole to proof and possibly correct. This costs you less, but gives the printer at least one or two proofs per print form to do the settings on their machines.

Why should you do colour corrections at the repro studio? After all, a book or a magazine isn't sold in shops with standardized lighting.

Have you ever come back from a trip to Africa or Asia with beautiful batik fabrics that looked amazing when you were there, but that don't look so fabulous on your sofa? That's normal, because light radiates in a very different way in Africa than in European latitudes, and the colours printed on cotton whose texture has not changed one iota in the aircraft hold inevitably give off different vibrations.

During the prepress phase, if you look at the image at home on your poorly calibrated screen, and then you subsequently work on it at your repro studio, where you're given a proof calibrated under standardized light, and you check a second proof next to your window on a rainy day (or on a sunny summer afternoon), you are very probably not looking at the same thing. The best way to guarantee successful image reproduction is to follow a coherent process. It is therefore preferable, especially for subjects where colour accuracy is a priority, to carry out all the checks with your repro specialist in their studio under the same conditions and standardized light (5500° K/9440° F) so the monitoring is consistent from start to finish. This will enable the printer to work objectively with the same parameters.

be used for printing. If your files are mediocre or vary in quality, explain what your priorities are: for example, bright colours, legibility, contrast, sharpness, descreening, specific retouches.

It is important to indicate generally, or sometimes document by document, what you wish to enhance or erase in an image, and what needs to be retained at all costs in other cases.

IMAGE BACKGROUNDS

Image backgrounds are frequently used, for example, in food photography, sculpture catalogues for art galleries or furniture, cosmetics, and jewellery brochures. It is advisable to give instructions on the precise tonality (warm, cold, neutral) of the backgrounds and possible unification when there are different tonalities and densities in your documents.

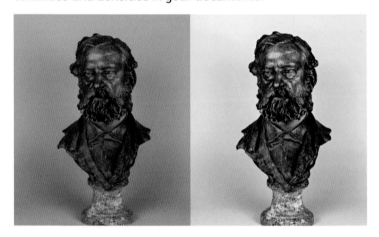

Reproduction fidelity

A good Photoshop operator can go (almost) as far as you want, but it's up to the person who has commissioned the job to know how far to push when transforming or interpreting an image and where to stop. This decision should take into account the subjectivity of our vision, our emotions, and our commercial objectives.

Proofs marked with specific instructions for colour correction and retouching.

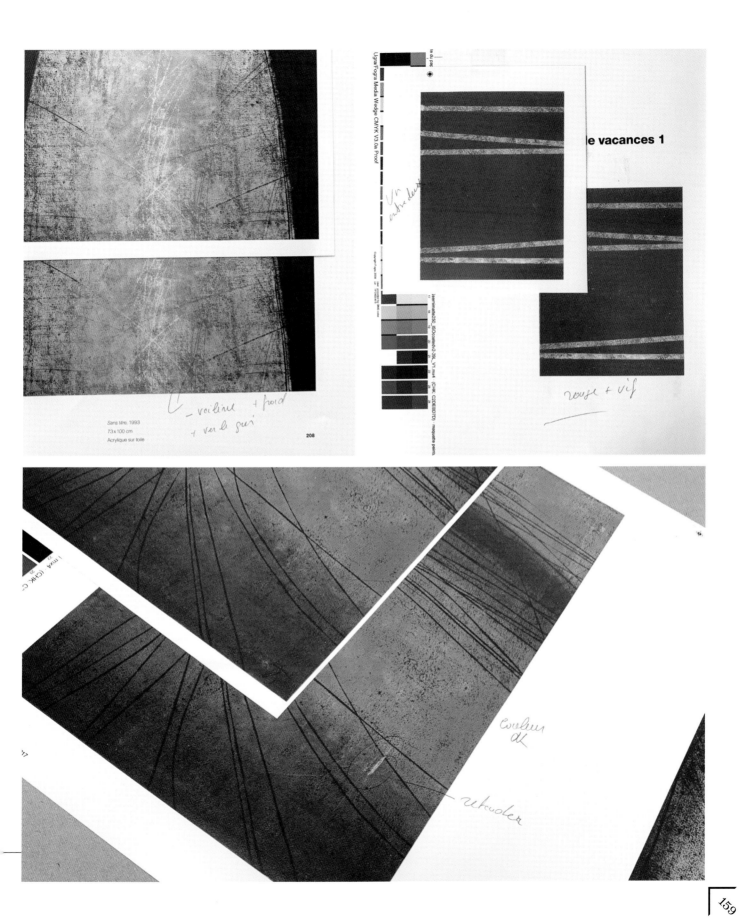

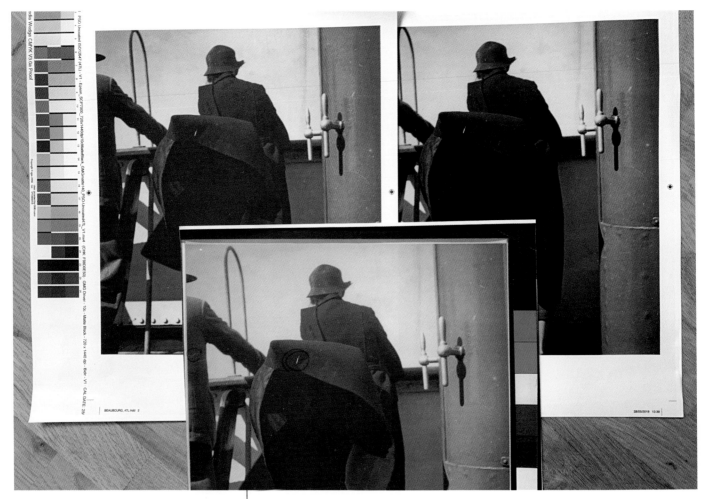

How far should you go to correct the 'defects' of an old original?

Some preliminary work is desirable when reproducing certain subjects, especially when the sources are of dubious quality: opaque documents, screened documents, scans of transparencies or prints.

But what approach should you take for shots by famous photographers or images of celebrities: should you retouch defects in the print, should you alter the image based on a particular principle? You shouldn't leave it up to your operator to make this kind of decision. This is a huge responsibility and is a decision for the client, not the colour specialist. Any decision should be based on the message you're trying to convey. It's not up to the operator to take it on themselves to delete details of whatever size in an illustration; indeed, you could be sued for changing a Cartier-Bresson photograph even slightly because he has left to posterity only prints approved and signed by himself ('the work is the print'). In this case, the repro professional will be working under the watchful eye of the rights holders. But if a publisher demands absolute and uncompromising fidelity to a Japanese print, you can always reply that countless different versions and copies were printed in the past using old and relatively unstable techniques.

Finally, once the repro expert has taken into account the subjectivity of your instructions and corrected any discrepancies related to the nature and state of preservation of the documents received, they begin **the essential part of their work, namely, faithfully reproducing a document and, above all, making it printable**.
Printing succeeds if the paper, the ink and the way the file has been prepared for these two materials are properly matched.

Prepare a document for printing

As mentioned earlier, the ICC profile enables an RGB file to be correctly transferred to a CMYK file and then to CMYK suitable for a specific stock. This is particularly important when working on uncoated stock, because the screen type, the lines per inch, the density and above all the total ink coverage (superposition rate of the four colours) will be very different. Therefore you cannot simply give the printer CMYK files; the question is, which CMYK?

The smaller the dot, the more subtle and precise the lines and shades of colour become. However, this is far from being an absolute truth because the accuracy of the dot and the lines is directly related to the nature of the substrate, which absorbs ink dots differently, more or less 'crushing' them onto the sheet through the pressure applied by the blanket.

These days, that's where most of a repro professional's expertise lies. They know how to adapt the profile to paper types that are coloured and 'closed' to different degrees; **they have to anticipate how the ink will behave on a given material and deal with expected deviations in colour and definition** (opening up details in dark areas of the subjects printed on uncoated paper or a textile, for example).

They know how to determine the definition and resolution according to the type of printing: a file for a subway poster consisting of 12 print forms on a 70 × 100 offset press is very different from a file for the same-sized plastic tarpaulin printed on a large-format digital plotter.

Checklist
COORDINATE THE REPRO

- **Ask for the date you need to deliver the PDFs to the printer and draw up a schedule with the repro studio.**

- **Supply repro with a page layout file or rough framing of the other documents.**

- **Analyze and comment on the documents.**

- **Indicate the retouches to be done: cut-out, adding material and colour corrections.**

- **Indicate the printing paper (uncoated, coated; white, very white, coloured).**

- **Work as much as you can in consistent light conditions.**

2

Prepress

Each type of printing and each substrate requires specific file preparation. But depending on your projects there are other adjustments to be made that also require graphic skills.

The final hurdle before printing

The overall quantity of ink for the four layers taken together, called total area coverage (TAC), is set in the prepress phase based on the appropriate ICC profile for the paper type. Once this parameter has been set, it is easier for the printer to adjust the density, i.e., the quantity of ink to release from the ink reservoir to the sheet via the plate and blanket, with the pressure calibrated accordingly. Everything is connected. Trust your partners: tell them what you want and leave them to do these settings. But if you are preparing your files without using a repro specialist, these are the points you need to watch out for:

– **Superposition rate**: for images, you need to adhere to the maximum superposition rate for each paper type: 300 to 350% maximum for high-quality coated paper; 270% maximum for uncoated paper, because the lack of coating causes the ink to spread and cause more dot gain, which is why we plan for less inking on 'open' paper (see page 98).

– **The ICC profile**: get the FOGRA profile for your paper stock from the

Right, an image processed with a 300% superposition rate for printing on coated paper, left, with a 270% rate for uncoated paper (see page 194).

printer and apply it to your images before creating your PDFs. The printer adjusts the line screen based on the paper for the same reasons: too many lines means too many dots that end up being too close together or joined to one another, invading areas that require few or no dots to reproduce light colours and details (reminder: 133 LPI is used for newspapers, while 175 LPI is standard for books).

Preparing a file for a different language

You are producing a publication for which you need several versions in different languages. In an ordinary file, the text (100% black) and the halftone screen black of the illustrations are combined on the same layer. **So the printer can change the language, you need to produce a base file with the four CMYK layers for the illustrations placed on their image layer, and a separate file for the text that you call text black.**

The printer will put the black base layer with each language to produce a new black plate each time containing the black text and the halftone screen black of the images. **Separating the text layer means that only one plate needs to be changed each time, reducing the makeready costs**.

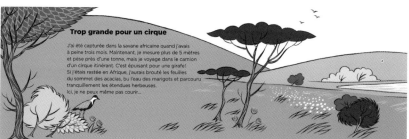

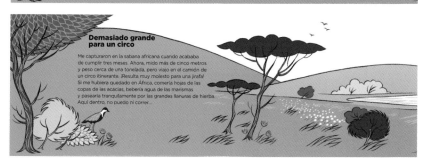

BANANA SKIN

If you have colour text, you will have to change all the relevant plates for each form. This requires recalibrating the registration and colour each time, making a change of language very costly. However, if your text is white, all the underlying layers are knocked out. A language change is usually done by changing the text on the single black plate that overprints. This is called a 'black plate change'.

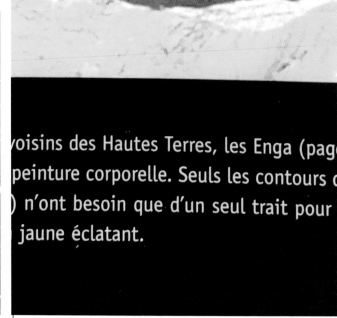

1 | 2

There are two ways you can change language with negative text on a black background.
1) The first method is to switch from positive to negative: instead of printing black text on a white background, you put the text in a white space on a 100% black background; you only change one plate, but the disadvantage is that this single black, with no four-colour support, is never very deep.
2) The other method consists of knocking out the black as previously described and adding a light solid colour to the entire black background so that you get a tint in a sufficiently legible shade in the text space. In this way, you achieve a 'strong' and therefore more intense black while only changing one plate.

Registration of the four colours, and the pressure, density and colour settings stay virtually unchanged every time the machine is stopped, and only a small calibration is required for the black registration.

Managing the halftone screen

In prepress, a continuous tone is transformed into a set of screens that, when superimposed in four-colour printing, give the best possible simulation of the original.
This screen, as we've seen, is made up of a greater or lesser number of larger or smaller dots that are closer or further away from each other. They are arranged in lines and angled in different ways to avoid conflict between the four CMYK colour screens.

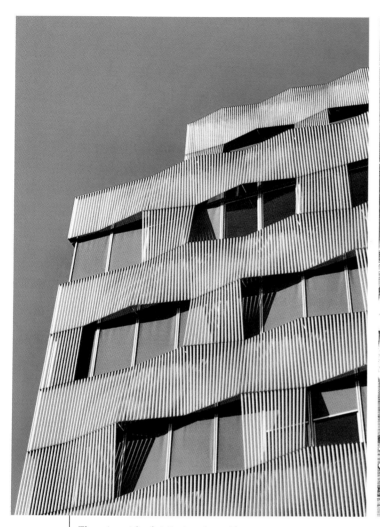

There is a risk of stair stepping with this image.

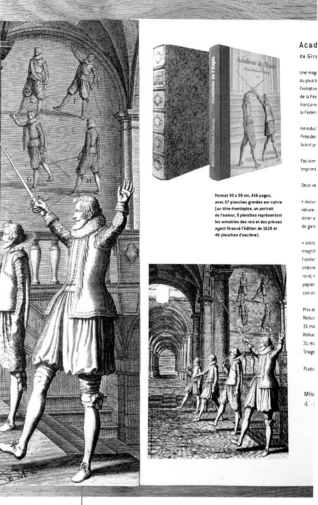

Format 30 x 38 cm, 416 pages,
avec 57 planches gravées sur cuivre
(un titre-frontispice, un portrait
de l'auteur, 8 planches représentant
les armoiries des rois et des princes
ayant financé l'édition de 1628 et
46 planches d'escrime).

An example of moiré on a photogravure.

The work done in repro consists of avoiding some of the disadvantages related to the behaviour of these screens.

The geometric nature of a screen can come into conflict with the nature of the object being reproduced. When reproducing images of architectural structures, furniture or any geometry with horizontal, vertical or oblique lines, you can end up with two screens that are superimposed, creating a **stair-stepping** effect.

The screens then need to be orientated in such a way as to prevent two superimposed angles.

The most common problem is **moiré**, which is caused by the presence of a screen in the original documents (reproductions printed in letterpress or offset) whose original screen interferes with the final screen of your work. This problem arises when we reproduce rugs, a print, fabrics with

Orientation of the four CMYK screens.

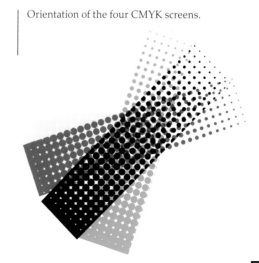

An image that is originally screened or that contains superimposed screens is likely to suffer from moiré.

fine but visible weft, and also documents that were already originally screened (cuttings from newspapers and printed books).

In traditional repro before DTP existed, you could counteract this by trying to orientate the lines of screen dots in such a way as to prevent the screen angles and detailed image networks coming too close together. These problems can no longer be solved in this way, because screen angles are not done specifically for each image but globally for all CTP print forms. Moreover, in the past, proofs were produced from the same technologies as the printing (films and plates), whereas these days control proofs are produced using digital inkjet printers that simulate as best they can the visual result and the paper stock to be used in printing, but not the screen or the inks.

If you have a major doubt about an entire job, the solution might be to use random screening.

> ✳ TIP
> **For sensitive jobs with a risk of moiré, it is advisable to allocate a small budget to do a test print at the printers. Only genuine offset screens can show up a defect that might not be visible on a digital proof.**

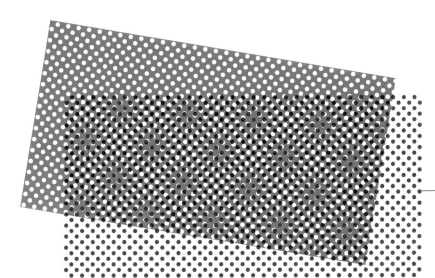

Principle of moiré with two superimposed screens.

STOCHASTIC OR RANDOM SCREENING

Conventional screening consists of superimposing four screens for the four colours, each made up of dots of varying size arranged in regular lines.

In four-colour printing, the screens for the three strong colours are angled at 30° to one another so they don't interfere with each other, which would cause moiré. The higher the line screen, the finer the details that can be reproduced in the image. In random or 'stochastic' (Greek: that which occurs by chance) screening, clouds of tiny, same-sized dots fall randomly where they are needed, a bit like a spray, in greater or larger numbers in a given area depending on the density required for the image being reproduced. This technique eliminates the moiré problems associated with the geometry of conventional screens and allows very fine details to be reproduced (highlights in jewellery, for example). However, it requires greater control of inks and paper via the production of highly sensitive plates, with quality dependent on the printer's CTP rather than the repro work. The disadvantage of random screening is that it is harder to reproduce the depth, volume and density of images; it also emphasizes the slightest defect in an image.

Mixed screens have been favoured for some time, as they combine the finesse of stochastic in the light and dark parts of an image, while traditional screening brings contours and contrast to the midtones.

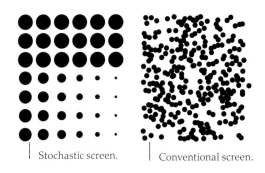

Stochastic screen. Conventional screen.

How many colours can I print?

Whether it's a rotogravure press, a web offset press or a sheet-fed machine, you will always have at least four units with four ink reservoirs for the four primary colours: cyan, magenta, yellow and black (CMYK). When mixed, these four colours can produce nearly all (with the emphasis on 'nearly') the colours or at least come as close to them as possible.

We won't be dealing here with web presses that struggle to manage an extra colour because the fifth unit is mainly used for a protective varnish. **Sheet-fed offset presses often have a fifth unit with an ink reservoir in which you can put either a varnish or a spot colour**; this is not possible in digital printing, where you print with digital-specific toner cartridges or inks.

On offset presses, you can have up to 10 ink reservoirs. This means you can print nearly all the visible colours with a palette of four primary colours, to which Pantone spot colours can be added. Specific inks can be used to extend the gamut, i.e., the relatively limited spectrum of four-colour printing.

Why do you sometimes have to extend this palette?

In everyday life and in the dictionary, there is a colour called orange. We have already seen that not all colours exist in all languages and that colours are not always constant in the history of a civilization, but let's accept the convention that anyone who can see a particular optical vibration can use the word 'orange' to refer to a frequency somewhere between yellow and red on a cathode-ray tube.
There are two ways we can translate this frequency onto a sheet of paper:

1 – A composite colour (CMYK tint):
The plates on a printing press will look for the primary colours to transfer them onto the blanket that then transfers them onto the sheet. In the case of orange, the yellow and magenta inks are superposed in different percentages, and the press operator must ensure the colour mix remains consistent throughout the print run. Following the same principle, we mix yellow and cyan to obtain green; magenta, yellow and black for burgundy, and so on. A colour tint chart provides the percentages for each shade of colour that can be reproduced by superposing 1, 2, 3 or 4 colours. You'll notice that sometimes you cannot reproduce an exact hue, especially when it

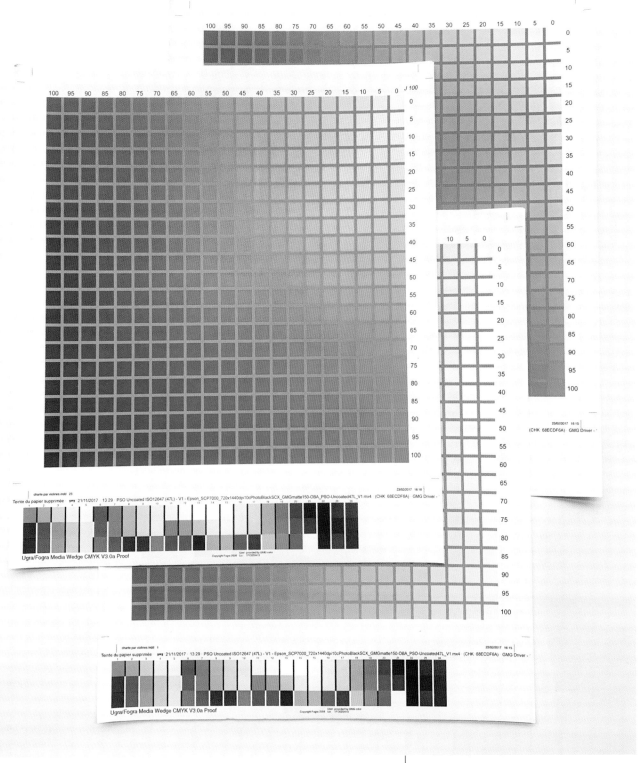

Composite colour charts to find a specific colour in four-colour printing.

BANANA SKIN

Can we always find the four-colour equivalent of a Pantone?
Some Pantones are more or less reproducible in four-colour, others not at all. Bear this in mind when you're creating a logo or a corporate style guide, because if you choose a non-convertible Pantone, you or your client will be forced to print in five colours (or more) every time. If all you're doing is printing paper bags or press kits, you can get by with one Pantone or two plus black for the text, but as soon as you need to publish a brochure, catalogue or book, or even an advert in a magazine (printed on a web press and therefore using a four-colour process), the presence of a colour that cannot be converted for use in four-colour printing causes a problem.

comes to bright or fluorescent colours. In this case, you have the option to use an additional ink called Pantone.

2 – A spot colour (Pantone):

You can pre-mix a specific ink to put in an ink reservoir and reproduce, for example, a very precise orange that remains stable over the course of one or several print runs over a period of time, as long as it is always printed at the same density.

Pantone 811

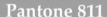

Four-colour Orange
M70 + Y100

Left, the jacket in four-colour printing; and right, the cover in spot colours.

Use a Pantone colour chart
to find the exact colour.

CHOOSE THE RIGHT PANTONE

PANTONE is an American company established in the mid-nineteenth century to manufacture colour charts for cosmetics. A century later, the company invented the Pantone Matching System (PMS) and began selling prefabricated inks to printers so they could reproduce certain shades with a high degree of accuracy.

A colour is obtained by mixing the inks before they reach the printing machine. Pantone inks are made from eighteen base colours including black, the three primary inks of four-colour printing (cyan, magenta, yellow) and a transparent white to make the other colours lighter.

There are three Pantone colour charts depending on the stock you are using. This notion is very important, because the light reflected by the printed surface and the shade of colour changes depending on how absorbent the paper is.

Always be precise when you give Pantone references, specifying whether you want:

Pantone XXX**C** (coated), for semi-matt and glossy coated paper;

Pantone XXX**M** (matt), for solid matt coated paper;

Pantone XXX**U** (uncoated), for uncoated paper.

BANANA SKIN

Don't make the mistake of imagining that a Pantone in the C range has an identical twin in the U range. Sometimes the same reference leads to significant discrepancies: if you have planned to use exactly the same colour on a book cover printed on coated paper and the inside of a book printed on uncoated paper, check the colours by comparing the two colour charts side by side. Sometimes, you'll need to move up a tone in the U range or even use the adjacent reference: uncoated paper absorbs more ink (and light) and dulls the final result by altering certain hues. In the example above, different Pantones were used to obtain the same colours on the uncoated paper inside the book and the coated paper on the cover: yellow 3959U and blue 315U for the inside, yellow 101C and blue 316C for the cover.

Teinte du papier supprimée   06/01/2020 14.24 PSO Uncoated (ISO12647 (47L) - V1 - Epson_SCP7000_720x1440dpi10cMatteBlack_GMGmatte140_PSO-Uncoated47L_V1.mx4 (CHK F98D0E50) GMG Driver - 10c

Ugra/Fogra Media Wedge CMYK V3.0a Proof

* TIP

How do you print a specific colour on coloured paper?

There's only one reliable solution: screen printing. The inks cover well and do not come into conflict with the colour of the paper, which is the case in offset where inks are 'transparent'. It's also possible to pre-print a white that covers well on a digital press or an offset HUV/LED press.

If you absolutely must print a Pantone on colour paper on an offset press, you will have to make some very precise technical adjustments – or, more accurately, adjust through trial and error. To obtain a given colour, you need to have the paper colour analyzed on a spectrometer, 'subtract' the value of the required Pantone composition and find a different Pantone, which is probably lighter, and, when added to the value of the colour of the paper, will ultimately give the colour you were looking for.

Working with Pantone enables a given colour to be reproduced consistently and almost perfectly, which is very important in the textile, cosmetics and many other sectors. Some brands are identified by a precise colour, and they need to reproduce their products or elements of their brand identity with total accuracy; the red soles of Louboutin shoes and Barbie pink are set in stone thanks to Pantone references. Nowadays, you can calibrate your computer screen on the Pantone colour chart and offer a complete colour reproduction process, which is sometimes a major contractual issue with clients.

Special cases

1– White: White is an absence of colour: it's the place where no ink is deposited on the sheet because there is no dot on the plate corresponding to a printable dot.

White is a 'hole', because there is no information in the source file. In graphic arts jargon, we refer to this as 'knockout' (blank text on a coloured background). White in this case is the colour of your printed substrate. You might want to glance back at the chapter on paper (see pages 88 to 92) to find out about the secrets and pitfalls of this supposed non-colour. You cannot print white on offset or gravure; it can be done with a specific ink in screen printing, a white ink in digital printing and in offset only on HUV/LED presses.

Black paper printed in four-colour thanks to a white ink backing

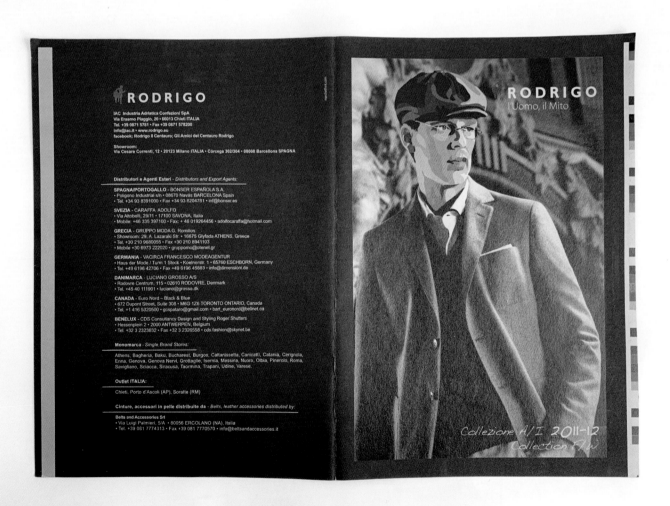

White screen print on black paper.

If you don't import your text correctly into the layout, the black text may end up being in four colours, which makes registration almost impossible.

You need to make sure that the black you import is black only, and not 'four-colour', 'registration' or 'RGB'.

The same principle applies to drawings or diagrams in black. Coloured text is possible, but you must keep an eye on this to avoid misregistration issues. Text in a tint is also not recommended if you want to print a product in several languages in succession. Refer back to the instructions for changing language (page 163).

2– Colour text: If you are digital printing, you can reproduce text in composite colours more easily, even small-sized text; the dots are squarer and the screen sharper, which significantly reduces registration problems. In offset, it is harder to match tiny details to within a micron because of the double transfer from plate to blanket and blanket to paper. Getting registration of the four colours right is one of the greatest limitations of traditional printing, which is why **four-colour text shouldn't be printed in offset or gravure.**

What are the right conditions for printing colour text?
Composite shades consisting of two colours and text with large enough fonts will work.

Here is an example of well-registered (left) and poorly registered (right) two-colour text; the size of the printed sheets, the position of the page on the sheet or a simple lack of attention from the printer can cause these variations in the same work.

Registering text in a tint becomes even more complicated with serif typography, very small point sizes and when there are too many colours. The size of the press also comes into play: on large-format presses, paper curling at the edges due to the heat and the movement of the sheets accentuates any registration difficulties.

A knockout text on a colour or four-colour black background will pose the same problems for obvious reasons: background colours that aren't perfectly registered will overlap into the knockout area, causing an unsightly effect. In this case, consider trapping, a technique that consists of slightly enlarging the knockout areas so that the underlying three-colour printing doesn't encroach on the white space. The same applies to coloured elements inserted on a tint background: enlarging the embedded element avoids the gap between it and the background that can cause a white border to appear between the two.

The pages in the same book have not all been registered in the same way.

126

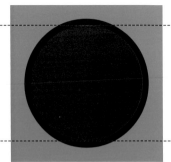

Incorrect alignment of cyan and magenta.	Trapping: the magenta area is slightly larger than the cyan opening in which it is placed.	Trapping: the cyan opening is slightly smaller than the magenta area.	Centred: both areas are trapped in the same proportions.

The white text space on a blue background is not a problem. But registration problems occur when other colours are added to the composition.

Using uncoated paper throws up even more obstacles, because the impact is not so clean and the ink more diffuse, making any registration problems more obvious.

3– Black: We obtain black by transferring black ink onto a sheet; the black looks black when it is text, but on solid colours it appears dark grey-brown, possibly flecked, especially if it is screened (see page 53).

How do you get a good, dense black background? The recipe for a neutral and balanced black is: 100K + 35C, 35Y, 35M. You can also obtain a deep black in a colder tone with 100% black and 40% cyan. There's no point going beyond that: more ink won't improve the visual perception and you run the risk of exceeding the permitted inking rate by causing,

RÉVÉLATIONS

DÉSINTÉGRATION

...ATION

Using a Pantone is particularly interesting for solid colours because it's more stable and uniform than a tint. The difference is even more noticeable on a screened background: here 70% black vs Pantone Cool Grey 10C in the foreground.

SUPER-BLACK

Vantablack, or super-black, is a carbon nanotube-based pigment that blocks even the slightest reflection of light and absorbs 99.965% of visible light. This results in the darkest black ever obtained and produces astonishing effects when applied to objects. The artist Anish Kapoor caused controversy by buying the patent in 2016, which raised ethical issues in the art world and beyond; luckily, there is a publicly available formula that is used in screen printing.

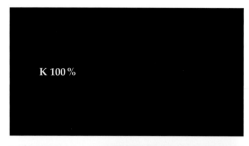

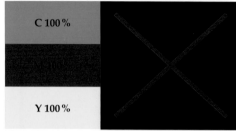

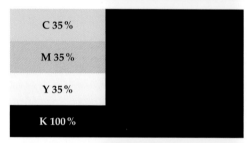

at the very least, set-off, and in the worst case the ink being rejected. The superposition rate of the four inks is one of the basic prepress settings; it is related to the type of paper and the machine but also to the nature of the inks used. Remember that it is usually between a minimum of 270% for printing on uncoated paper and a maximum of 300 to 350% on coated paper. **Ask your printer what the maximum superposition rate is for your particular stock** and – we can't repeat this enough – pass this vital information on to your repro service.

Checklist
COORDINATE PREPRESS

- **Name documents and never change the reference.**
- **Integrate the images into the layout file (update).**
- **Be careful never to leave images in RGB or in low resolution.**
- **Have screened/halftone images or images with fine screens checked.**
- **Check the enlargement rate of the images.**
- **Check bleeds; provide all fonts.**
- **Pay attention to the size of colour borders and text; restrict the number of colours in small-size text or borders.**
- **Plan trapping for knockout text on a colour background.**
- **Choose the Pantone according to the printing paper.**
- **Plan a fifth layer for a spot colour.**
- **Plan a fifth layer for a change of text when printing several languages in a row.**
- **Produce or have produced certified PDFs; approve them on a screen or a laser proof before sending to the printer**

3
Printing

You'll rarely get the chance to visit a gravure press; it is even less likely that you'll get to climb up one of its fascinating towers whose impressive size, noise and very distinctive ink smell can be intoxicating.

You may get the opportunity to go into a commercial printing plant. With the reels rolling at speed, the splattered papers piling up and the busy undershirt-clad operator, it's an atmosphere somewhat reminiscent of the film *Modern Times*.

You're more likely to have your baptism of fire beneath an offset press. I hope you do, because it's a fascinating experience during which you very quickly understand everything you struggled to learn on the school bench in your physics and chemistry lessons.

If you're planning to watch the start-up of the printing process, bear in mind that most of the work will have been done during the prepress phase and you won't be able to substantially change the final result. **You'll never get a good printed result with poor repro, but, if your files are correctly prepared, you can bring that extra touch to your work once it's on the machine, with the operator's help.**

How to work with the printer

– You have received a detailed quote – and potentially negotiated on price – and agreed a schedule for file submission and delivery dates, a blank dummy or paper samples.
– You have ordered the paper and booked a slot for your printing.
– **You are going to issue a purchase order containing the terms and conditions of the quote you have accepted and the schedule.** If your printer is in another city or country, agree with them who pays for the shipping of the material and for the travel expenses to attend the press checks and give approval for printing.
– Respect the terms of payment: if you have been asked for an advance, send it by bank transfer to be sure that the paper is ordered and the job scheduled.
– On the agreed day, **send your files and proofs**. If you are unable to keep to the planned date, don't wait until the last minute to tell the printer, who will do their best to amend the schedule to suit everyone.
– Follow the detailed schedule you are sent and approve the **final plotter proof to give the go-ahead for printing on the scheduled date**.
– Once the sheets have been printed, check everything carefully and **give the green light for the finishing so the printer can continue production**. Be aware that some errors can still generally be put right at this stage. In the event of a major problem, it's still possible to limit the damage by reprinting all or part of the job before the sheets are folded, the signatures assembled, a cover attached and the object finished.
– **Quickly confirm the delivery addresses** with the phone numbers of the various recipients, opening hours and unloading details (delivery in a city centre is not the same operation or the same cost as delivery to a warehouse with a loading bay).

THE AWKWARD QUESTION

When should I supply the proofs to the printer?

Clients often turn up at the printers on the day of printing with their proofs tucked under their arm, but it is advisable to provide them beforehand to give your printer a chance to examine them. If you're printing on coated paper, your files should have a profile for coated paper – FOGRA 39 or 51 – and the proof paper should be glossy or satin. Conversely, for uncoated paper, the profile used is FOGRA 47L or 52, and your proofs on matt paper should simulate an uncoated paper. Nevertheless, when the printing paper is a high bulk matt art, the printer can adapt the workflow and the line screen in order to optimize the curves based on the subjects reproduced on your proofs.

- **Approve the sample copies** you receive before the goods are shipped. This is the recommended approach, because a minor oversight or an instruction that wasn't passed on can still be dealt with at this juncture (shrink-wrapping, labels, etc.).

At their end, the printer acknowledges receipt and provides a schedule detailing dispatch of the following items:
- Soft (screen) or hard (paper) plotter proof, final deadline for your approval. (Bear in mind that a plotter is simply used to approve imposition and not to rewrite your text at the last minute.)
- The correct sheets for the different elements: inside block, cover, etc.
- A few finished copies, one or two days before delivery.
- A packing list at the time of delivery.
- An invoice in accordance with your purchase order.

Make sure you are available and can be contacted throughout the production period (one to three weeks for a magazine, four to five weeks for a book). Bear in mind that any delay in giving your approval leads to slippage in your schedule that could compromise the smooth running of operations.

The printer is in charge of a series of jobs – prepress and plate preparation, printing, folding, finishing, binding, packaging and shipping – which all need to be scheduled internally or with external subcontractors. You need to understand what these jobs involve and do everything required of you in a timely fashion to ensure the printer can meet the agreed deadlines.

HOW TO MANAGE ADDITIONAL COSTS

If additional costs arise, the printer should provide a figure without delay and you should give your explicit approval. Both sides need to react quickly, because bureaucracy should never block production. Make sure you can deal with this kind of situation either by taking the necessary decisions quickly yourself or by making sure your boss or client reacts promptly.

The same image in lines
and greyscale.

Which machines for how many colours?

One colour is enough for you: black (well, maybe not...). There are monochrome and web presses that print only black text (novels, for example), possibly accompanied by line illustrations (diagrams, sketches, certain basic prints). These function the same way as the typography, i.e., files whose structure consists only of yes/no data: either white or 100% black. The dots that make up these text elements or vector lines are very close together, don't have a true screen, and consequently contain no shades of grey.

These machines have a fairly high dot gain, but this is of no consequence, as we are looking for good black density and a sharp line without having to worry about gradation.

If your text is accompanied by illustrations such as black and white photographs or drawings that require transitions between black and white, you need to print halftones, i.e. single-colour greyscale images, where the gradation is conveyed by the size of the dots and the distance between them. There are web presses and small sheet-fed machines with less dot gain that can print the line of the text and the screen for the illustrations.

MANGA, AN ART IN ITSELF

Manga is printed in a single colour. This is a fascinating case that appears simple but is actually complex and requires considerable technical experience. The drawings are done by combining line drawings and screentone transfers of bigger or smaller dots.

These screentones were traditionally created manually but are now done on a computer. Moiré issues can occur depending on how fine they are and the enlargements or reductions they undergo. To prevent this, processing in greyscale should be avoided; to keep the screentone regular, you need to work in Bitmap (black and white without gradation) saved in TIFF. The print will be successful if the machine strikes forcibly and you are using an oil-based black, which can have a warmer or cooler colouration depending on the underlying paper. For example, if you want good contrast on yellowish paper, a blue-black is better than a brown-black.

A photograph reproduced
in duotone: a skeleton
black and a halftone for
the Pantone colour.

For a publication, **you can choose to print a signature with text using a Pantone navy blue, brown, bottle green or any colour dark enough to remain legible**, but not too dark either, because what remains perceptible as solid colour is perceived by the eye as black when applied to text.

You need several colours:
– Two colours (duotone)
This consists of a single black and white image that is shown in Photoshop as two nominal layers of inks (Pantone or four-colour) whose curves can be adapted at will to obtain the required rendering.
In Photoshop, you can choose 'Pantone' as the second colour (but note that Pantone is no longer supported in Photoshop without a subscription).
You can simply use the four-colour process inks to create duotones, or Pantone inks for a more sophisticated approach, as is the case with artworks that reproduce black and white photographs.

– Three colours
As you have four units at your disposal, treat yourself: if the subject justifies it, work on your photos in three colours using a four-colour black, a Pantone black (denser) and the accompanying colour in the Pantone grey ranges. This is the most subtle and the highest-quality processing, but you need a good repro specialist to create this type of file. There is one other limitation when it comes to using this age-old skill: only tests printed on the real machine with the real paper can really capture the result. A digital proof will not suffice.

THE CASE OF THE DUOTONE

Duotone or two-colour printing is the ideal process for printing black and white photographs. Your repro expert selects two layers: a well-designed halftone including the details that will be the black layer, and a second layer for the Pantone that is chosen from different tones of grey (Cool Grey, Warm Grey, etc.). The Pantone reinforces the blacks and feeds the highlights by bringing contours into the light colours and halftones. A third element can be used to enrich the whole: a dot-on-dot acrylic varnish (see page 192) that brings shine and depth to the blacks without flattening the overall effect.

BANANA SKIN

Pantone inks are more expensive and slow down the usual machine process, so don't be surprised if you are charged almost the same price for printing with two Pantone colours as you would be for four primary colours.

– Four colours

Four-colour printing is the classic process. **In CMYK, you can print any image you want in colour. This is by far the most common method for reproducing all kinds of colour images.**

You can also process black and white images in four-colour. This is particularly interesting for old documents where you want to keep the different tonalities.

Four-colour printing of old black and white documents, keeping the original tonalities.

Conversely, it is possible to process black and white documents in a stabilized four-colour process if you want to give a disparate collection of old documents a more uniform and precise tonality over an entire publication. The rendering is stabilized thanks to a subtle three-colour (trichromatic) process that nourishes the blacks and avoids the small fluctuations on machines that are sensitive to variations of around 2%. This gives you two advantages: as you are remaining in the CMYK sphere, you can add colour backgrounds and photos to your layout, all without increasing your budget owing to the cost of a fifth colour.

– Five colours
There are several possibilities:
- CMYK + a Pantone: you can use a combination of photos processed in four-colour and photos processed in duotone (black + Pantone). Pantone can also be used for backgrounds, which will remain very stable, as well as for typography.
- CMYK + a varnish (protection across the whole page, or selective) only on image blocks.
- 5 spot colours (rarer).

– Six colours
CMYK + two pure spot colours: **this is hexachromy, a technique developed by Pantone. It is used to expand the four-colour gamut by adding two fluorescent Pantones: orange + green, or orange + reflex blue.**
The orange is particularly bright, as are certain greens, violets or cobalt blues whose luminosity is difficult to reproduce in four-colour. Hexachromy gets closer to the purity and luminosity of the RGB spectrum of a bright screen, which is almost twice as wide as the CMYK spectrum.

– And more!
Some machines have six, eight, or even ten printing units, enabling you to print either five colours on both sides at the same time, as on a web press, or on one side after the other with the four-colour gamut enriched with spot colours and possibly varnish.

Four-colour reproduction of black and white documents in which the tonalities have been unified.

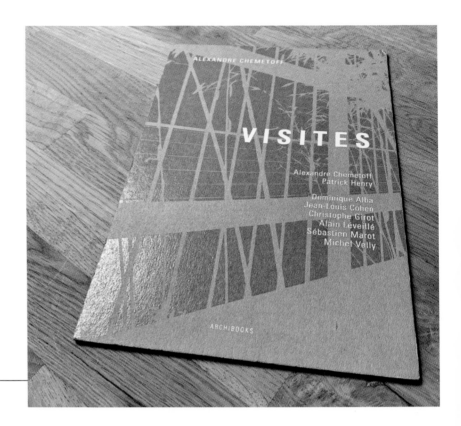

Opposite: grey board printed with a
varnish tinted with black ink.
Right: a selective inline varnish placed
only on the image blocks.

The case of varnishes

Offset 'inline', i.e. available in the fifth unit of an offset press, varnish can be used in different ways:

<u>Full-page</u> or <u>protective varnish</u>: this is applied to the full page to protect the entire surface from set-off – specks of dirt caused by the transfer of ink from one sheet or one page to another (see page 195). This can occur when sheets are stacked on the pallet as they leave the machine. It happens more often during the finishing phase, once the sheets are folded and assembled, when the block is passed under the trimming knife that trims all three sides. The pressure that the knife exerts on the edges of the block causes this ink transfer either because the ink isn't completely dry or because there is too much inking. Hence the importance of planning the superposition rate of the four colours in prepress to avoid any overload.

<u>Acrylic varnish</u>: this is an oilier transparent satin ink with a higher gloss than basic 'machine varnish'.

<u>Selective varnish</u>: this is when you apply a machine or acrylic varnish to the illustrations only rather than the whole page. Be careful: a single plate is used to varnish all the forms of the book for a full-page varnish,

but a fifth plate is needed for each form for a selective varnish, as a second file has to be created with image blocks for each page. This can incidentally serve to protect against set-off, but it is mainly an aesthetic effect to enhance images and make them stand out from the paper. A satin or shiny varnish should be chosen for a very matt coated paper, bearing in mind that a varnish is not as noticeable on glossy paper and is practically invisible on uncoated paper.

<u>Dot-on-dot varnish</u>: this works on the same principle as selective varnishing. In this case, a file is created in repro using only the black screen in the image block, which underlines, intensifies and reinforces the black by increasing the contrast and shininess in the dense tones.

USING VARNISH WISELY

Do you need to pay for a varnish just to prevent set-off? Don't imagine that varnish is an advantage in terms of quality. A printer who systematically varnishes is probably not the best in the world. Varnish tends to flatten the image, make the texture of the paper less noticeable and turn yellow over time; using it as a precaution is like saying speed is preferable to quality. Printers use varnish to fix the ink on the paper so they can proceed immediately to the finishing stage, but to achieve this you also need to use inks that dry relatively quickly, and the result may be a bit insipid. However, certain inks oxidize in air and dry naturally in one or two days while remaining on the surface of the paper. If you use these inks, you don't need varnish to 'fix' them, but you do need to allow time for this in the schedule. There is no need for varnish on a HUV/LED offset press where immediate drying eliminates any issues, especially for uncoated paper.

Ask for advice, look at the samples you are given and ask the right questions about varnish, making a clear distinction between the effects you're looking for and possible quality issues.

The physics and chemistry of printing

Computers mean that anyone can have a go at repro, but this is not the case in printing, where the issues are far more complex and the files have to be prepared correctly. Whereas in digital printing, the printed result is a sort of 'photocopy' of the file, **going from file to paper in the world of offset is a complex process** that needs to be carefully monitored to achieve a happy medium between standardization and subjectivity.

A printer therefore needs to process the files they receive very carefully, checking that the ICC profile is correct and that it matches the accompanying colour proofs; they then apply the appropriate line screen and engrave the plates.

We have seen that **offset printing is based on the principle of mutual repulsion of oil and water**. A blanket transfers the oily ink onto the paper from a plate on which printable dots have been engraved and where the flow of water and ink in the different areas is precisely regulated.

It is a delicate balance, as the two fluids must not be allowed to mix and emulsify. The printer adds reservoir solution, which is also necessary for the correct hygrometry of the paper, as well as adjuvants and solvents.

It is important to understand that **offset inks** do not work like gouache or paint for your walls. **They are transparent inks composed partly of pigments and partly of mineral and vegetable oil-based thinners and solvents.** The different gradations of colour result from an optical effect that occurs when screens of different dots are superimposed. The thinners are fixed first on the paper to ensure the ink 'takes'. This happens differently on different substrates: quickly on coated paper, slowly on uncoated 'open' paper, and not at all on plastic-based papers such as those used in flexography.

The layer of pigments associated with the mineral solvents and adjuvants stays on the surface and dries by oxidation upon contact with air. This is faster or slower depending on the ambient temperature and humidity, but also and primarily depending on each ink's chemical composition. 'Fresh' inks, designed to take more quickly, dry rapidly on the machine and avert set-off issues if you want to move quickly on to the folding stage. Inks that dry through oxidation reproduce the brilliance and intensity of colours even on uncoated paper because the pigments remain on the surface of the paper, but require drying time between printing each side of the sheets as well as before folding.

A printing sheet with colour bar showing the four full colours and the different screen percentages so the printer can check the densities are correct throughout the print run.

In the same way as the repro studio screen is calibrated according to light criteria, **the printer's press is calibrated according to density, pressure, dot gain and dampening. All of these criteria are based on standardized norms.**

On the sheets you see coming off the press, there is a colour bar that the operator constantly monitors using a densitometer. The colour bar (or strip) consists of small squares corresponding to the four basic CMYK colours and, if applicable, spot colours, in different screen percentages and therefore density. **Density measures the thickness of the ink layer on the paper**; on coated paper, the ink settles automatically on the surface, achieving good visual density without too much thickness; conversely, a lot more ink has to be deposited to achieve the same perception on stock that 'drinks' ink like uncoated paper, with the risk that the paper is over-soaked, hard to dry and set-off occurs. This problem cannot be solved at the last minute on the press but must be dealt with specifically in the prepress phase by reducing the superposition rate of the four ink layers; the total coverage is therefore lighter and good density can be obtained with fewer dots, fewer lines and, in short, less ink.

In parallel, for an uncoated stock where the absence of coating causes greater ink absorption and dot gain, the printer uses line screens that are less fine. As we saw on page 98, the right balance must be found between the paper, the pressure exerted by the blanket on the paper and the quantity (density) of ink to be used. If the overall quantity of ink for the four layers added together has been set correctly using the right ICC profile in the prepress phase, the press operator can adapt the line screen and tweak the quantity of ink and the pressure required according to the paper stock used. Everything is connected. Trust your partners: tell them what you want and let them make the adjustments that you do not have the skills to do. However, if you are the one preparing your files and the profiles, be aware of the intricacies of this stage.

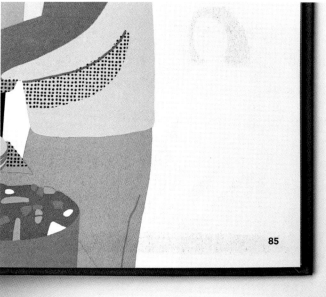

85

Example of set-off:
the black of the
hair is probably
overloaded with
the four colours.

Makeready and rolling

The plates are installed on the machine that is started up as the operator makes the following calibrations:

– pressure;

– density;

– registration, i.e., ensuring the four plates are perfectly aligned: the slightest shift might cause the image to blur as well as alter the general colour (see pages 176 to 178).

Once these preliminary settings are complete, the operator goes into more detail regarding colour considerations and calibrates the sheet with the help of the colour proofs, where the colour gamuts are used to help check the density of each colour, the grey balance and the white point.

Can you set up a sheet without colour proofs?

If no proofs are supplied to the printer, they will use established standards of pressure, density and registration: a standardized print that respects international standards is an acceptable-quality print.

Sometimes only a few sample proofs are provided for the entire job. These allow the machine operator to calibrate the sheet from the colour bars on these proofs without really going into any detail for each image, under the assumption that a consistent calibration for the images as a whole has been done in repro.

Once the main parameters have been set, the machine starts running; sheets are printed to make and check the settings. These sheets will not be used in the final publication and are called the **makeready sheets**. You may recall seeing that the printer's fixed costs include, among other things, a given quantity of paper that is used to calibrate the different machines on start-up (see page 126).

Once all the calibrations have been done and the printed sheets used for the press check set aside, the machine starts to run at full speed. While it's running, the operator does not stand idly by:

- They gauge the overall verisimilitude of the colours from features such as skin, the sky, greenery or certain objects.
- They monitor the consistency of solid colours, ensuring the hues are uniform and there are no hickeys, i.e., specks of dirt or scratches due to plate or blanket defects, which can still be rectified by replacing them. If certain background colours recur throughout a book, they make sure that these colours remain stable page after page and sheet after sheet. It is obviously easier to check the consistency of a colour when it is a Pantone, because it just needs to be printed at the same density everywhere. However, a four-colour halftone needs to be monitored more closely for overall balance between its constituent primary colours.
- They check the neutrality of the greys in certain image backgrounds to make sure a dominant one doesn't take over.
- They check the quality of the highlights and legibility of the details in the dense tones.
- They check the double-page spreads are all lined up: sometimes they are spread over different ink zones on the sheet, sometimes they even straddle two different sheets – lining up facing pages is one of the press operator's headaches. Sometimes an illustration needs an

✳ TIP
When printing on uncoated stock, defects sometimes appear that didn't jump out at you on the repro proofs: halos, irregularities in uniform colours, breaks in colour gradation or in a highlight, or even abnormal density. There is a way to find out whether the defect comes from the file or from your paper: ask your printer to slip a sheet or two of coated paper into the machine with the same settings. If the defects persist or are even more visible, it's your file causing the problem and the proof didn't bring this to light. But if the defects disappear, it's your paper that's the problem. A 'clogged' rendering on uncoated paper that appears normal on coated paper might indicate that you have given the printer files and proofs with the wrong profile.

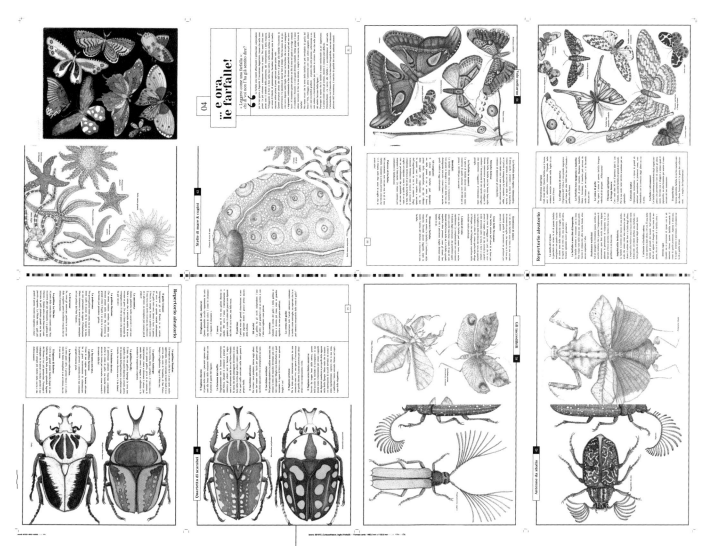

On the printing sheet, the two halves of the final double-page spread (top right) are not on the same ink zone…

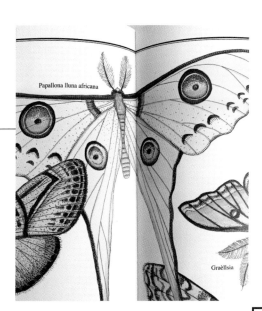

…but they have been correctly lined up.

extra density boost and this slightly alters the tonality of an image, the other half of which is on the ink zone of another image, which, conversely, could do with less ink density. The operator has to take an overall view of the job before making irreversible decisions. The larger the machine format, the more pages there are on a sheet and the more compromises have to be made, especially for the joins.

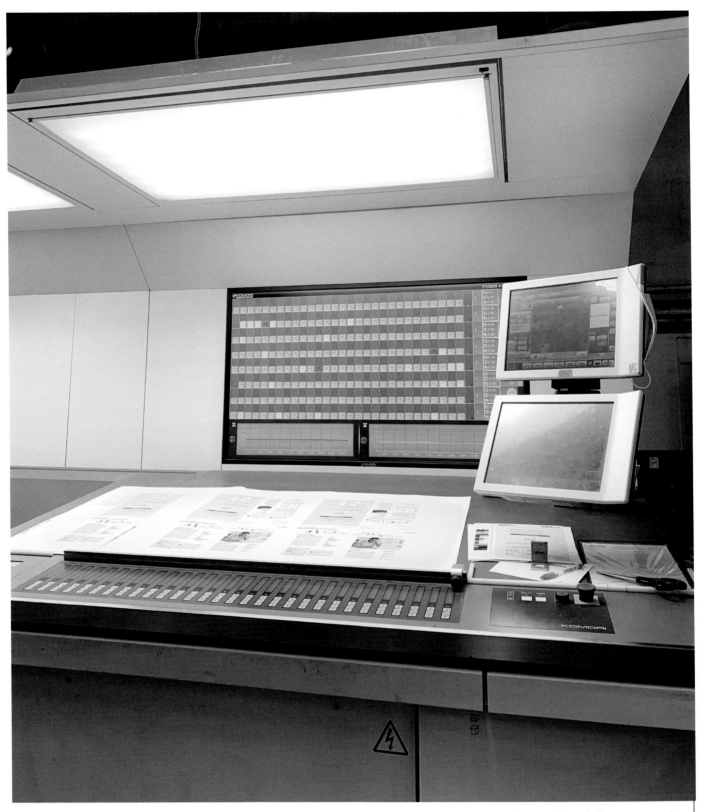

The control stand allows, among other things, the press operator to finely calibrate inking of the vertical strips.

How do you give approval at the printing press?

Once the machine operator has done their usual calibrations and checked it against your proofs, they might then present a sheet to the customer and allow some room for subjectivity: either yours or that of the end client you are representing. **This is where you can make comments, decide to change the contrast or use one tone rather than another for some images**; you can just express your overall feelings and let the operator make the necessary changes.

Standing in front of the machine and watching how fast it runs can be quite impressive and possibly slightly stressful. Think of this: the truth is in your files, and the colour proofs on the paper that simulates the print stock allow the press operator to get very close to the originals, but in no way, shape or form can you radically change on the machine what you have approved in the repro stage. Your room for manoeuvre when you're there in front of the printing press is limited to a few parameters:

– In photogravure, you work image by image, but on a press the pages are laid above and below one another in parallel strips on a sheet. The inking can be modulated across the width of the sheet, and the load of each colour can be controlled quite precisely by opening an ink reservoir to a greater or lesser degree on certain segments of the

BANANA SKIN

Beware: colours reduce slightly in intensity as they dry – especially on 'open' paper (uncoated or high bulk matt art), and you might be disappointed the day after you've approved your final press proofs. So don't reduce the densities too much if your printer strongly advises you not to when they are doing the makeready.

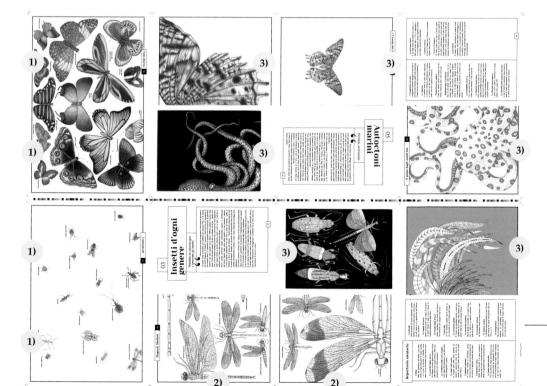

True doubles and doubles with their counterpart on opposite sides. On this sheet, there are three examples:
1) two true double-page spreads on the same ink zone of the sheet.
2) A join on two different ink zones on the sheet.
3) Six pages whose counterpart is on another sheet: the printer needs to set up the following sheets, making sure the joins for the six spreads are aligned.

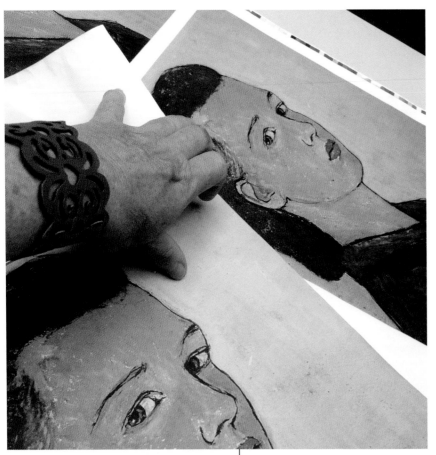

Here, the printer is guided
by the colour proof supplied
by the repro service.

sheet, which are called ink zones. You can only work in vertical strips. If you alter the density or the colour balance of an image, the whole strip is affected; from that point on, the art of the machine operator consists of finding a balance by making compromises between one image and another on the same strip in order to get as close to a proof as possible while respecting the overall coherence.

– You can ask for general adjustments to modify or accentuate the contrast, colour saturation, density of the blacks and so on. Be aware there are standards that set minimum and maximum density thresholds for each colour, so when your printer suggests not exceeding these, it's best not to insist. You risk overloading the sheet with ink or, conversely, getting a surprise once the ink has dried and lost some of its strength.

WHAT ARE MAKEREADY SHEETS?

Meanwhile, the machine is running and sheets are coming out that don't yet meet your requirements. The operator sets these sheets aside and only starts the real print run when you're fully satisfied with the result and you've signed the final proof on the sheet that suits you to give your approval. In printing jargon, the press check sheets that are reused for setting up subsequent sheets and for finishing operations are called makeready sheets. It is not impossible to come across some worrying defects on a print run: dirt, duplicated text, poor registration, and so on. Don't panic, but get your service provider to check this. It is likely that the bulk of your print run is in order and that a few makeready sheets have slipped through inadvertently in one or more copies, as they are removed manually and therefore subject to error.

This is one of the
four basic units
where the yellow
ink plate is found.

– If you're not satisfied with what you are presented with, don't get
upset and dig your heels in. Try to understand the explanations you
are given and avoid any obvious irritation with a machine that has a
rhythm to follow and with the operator in charge of it.

**The operator now monitors the consistent reproduction on the sheet
over the whole print run by taking regular samplings with a densitometer that show up any colour shift.**

Failures and fixes

A mantra to live by: Get advice and a price before you bin it. Sometimes
the stars are badly aligned on a particular production and trouble rears
its ugly head: obstacles to overcome, mistakes to admit to, alternative
solutions to find.

If you've done your checks at every stage and a defect has crept in
somewhere, raising doubts as to the quality of your product, you can
sometimes put the problem right during the production process, or maybe
even once the product is finished.

THE AWKWARD QUESTION

Can I change the type of paper during a print run?

Probably not. Stopping presses is
very costly, and the printer is
unlikely to want to do this, even if
they do have the desired paper.
Sometimes, you might be tempted if
you're not satisfied with the result,
but it all depends on how your
images have been processed and
your files constructed. If your
original intention was to print on
uncoated paper (open, porous) and
the profile used in prepress was
consistent with this, it means that
your printer has applied a 'loose'
line screen (175 LPI) and that coated
paper could be suitable for use here.
You probably won't get all the fine
detail, but you will get a more glossy
and highly coloured result than the
one on your proofs that were printed
on paper that simulates uncoated.
Conversely, if you had planned a
coated profile, your printer will have
used a much finer line screen (such
as 200 LPI), and therefore a larger
number of dots that will spread
abnormally on a porous paper such
as uncoated, leading to a dull,
excessively dense result, devoid of
detail and light.

If embossed paper poses a problem, as was the case in the image on the bottom right, as a last resort you can print on the reverse, i.e., the smooth side of the paper.

For example: you receive the correct sheets before finishing and you notice a major anomaly, either in the colour calibrations (the press operator didn't notice a double-page spread straddling two signatures), or in the text (just where the CEO has written her preface!), or in the page layout (a last-minute correction has disrupted the update of various elements and caused a font to disappear).

A thousand things can happen that don't necessarily mean you have to bin the entire print run. However, there are two issues that need to be addressed: how to rectify the error and who pays for it.

Responsibility is rarely a one-way street. Even if it was your graphic designer or repro person who slipped the wrong PDF into the pile while making a last-minute correction, the responsibility to check and approve each stage lies with you.

If your printer made the mistake, don't be too harsh. Just make sure they make up for the lost time by rectifying the error. If the mistake is yours, be as friendly as possible and see if the printer is willing to invoice just the material costs without any extra margin. In all cases, it is best to try and negotiate a way to (reasonably) share this extra cost.

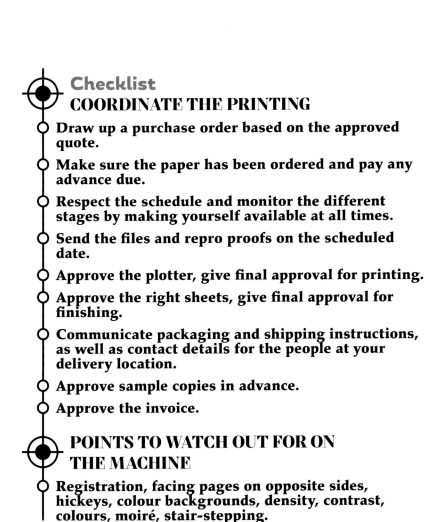

Checklist
COORDINATE THE PRINTING

Draw up a purchase order based on the approved quote.

Make sure the paper has been ordered and pay any advance due.

Respect the schedule and monitor the different stages by making yourself available at all times.

Send the files and repro proofs on the scheduled date.

Approve the plotter, give final approval for printing.

Approve the right sheets, give final approval for finishing.

Communicate packaging and shipping instructions, as well as contact details for the people at your delivery location.

Approve sample copies in advance.

Approve the invoice.

POINTS TO WATCH OUT FOR ON THE MACHINE

Registration, facing pages on opposite sides, hickeys, colour backgrounds, density, contrast, colours, moiré, stair-stepping.

4

Finishing

An interesting historical fact: the replacement of parchment by papyrus and then paper revolutionized the history of books. But well before that, another major transformation influenced the way books evolved: the replacement of scrolls by codexes in around 3 BCE.

The codex, made from one or several quires, finally gave readers the freedom to leaf through the object, and to be able to stop and resume reading. The fact that a text was folded meant that it could be indexed and consulted at will. **A codex was finished in the same way books are today** and freed readers from the continuous linear reading of scrolls, which were also fairly fragile, limited in capacity and inconvenient to store.

Just as some people today are critical of e-readers (even though it's handy to be able to take your entire library and all your dictionaries on holiday with you), and just as medieval Christians were wary of Sino-Arabic paper, the codex was long scorned by the intellectuals of antiquity and even banned outright by the priesthood of the time. However, early Christians, in their eagerness to propagate their ideas effectively, adopted this new technology and ensured its future through the dissemination of the Gospels.

Trimming a leaf...

...a four-pager...

...and a signature.
Note that this is the only way to free the leaves of a signature.

Trimming

The term 'finishing' means giving a printed object its final form. **Trimming is the first, and sometimes only, finishing operation depending on whether or not your product requires folding and assembly.**

Trimming is the essential part of the process to:

- eliminate the trim or bleed on the four sides of a single element that occupies the whole printing sheet, such as a large poster (that will stay flat), a sewing pattern or a road atlas (that will subsequently be folded);
- slit a sheet once or several times to separate individual elements: leaves that need to come off (postcards, small posters, flyers, etc.);
- trim a signature folded from a small sheet;
- slit a large sheet into strips that will be folded individually into several signatures;
- trim the three sides of a brochure once the signatures and cover have been assembled.

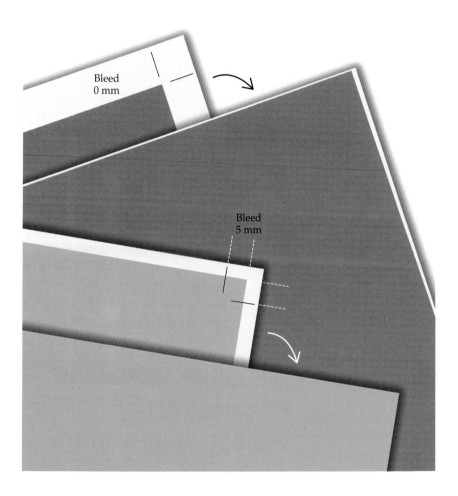

Bleed
0 mm

Bleed
5 mm

BANANA SKIN

The trim, as you will recall, is the 3 to 5 mm (³⁄₁₆ in) margin on all four sides of each element that will subsequently be separated; for example, a leaf or the double pages that will form a signature.

This space is important because the printer includes it in their imposition, and you should include it in your files for each page.

A trimmer is a mechanical device that has a known and tolerated margin of variation. If you glued postcards together, the knife would quite likely move and not cut exactly where it should, leaving a small strip of the adjacent image showing. Conversely, if a white margin were left around the image instead of letting it overlap, the knife might cut a bit further and leave a white line visible, which is why it is important to extend an image or colour background into the trim.

A folded signature assembled with a scored cover.

que ce ne soit l'un et
ctoires. De nouvelles
ent en question les
propre de l'animal
Paul Klee. Animalité
ervait un type de
ent, il inversait les
itoires de sa faune!

r relationship with
bilities of animals
nature of animals
hese issues in his art.
of the relationship
iour in animals
. Follow Klee's

lhöfer

Mittwoch **31. Oktober**
Halloween-Monster-
Auf den Spuren von H
Luft-Ungeheuern und
Für Gross und Klein

Sonntag **11. Novembe**
Kunst und Philosophi
Markus Wild, Professo
Philosophie Universitä
Gespräch mit Dominik
Kunstvermittlung ZPK

Sonntag **11. Novembe**
Das schlaue Füchslei
Von L. Janáček, Bearb
Konzert des Ensemble
Kaspar Zehnder, Flöte
Martina Jankova, Sopr

Sonntag **13. Januar 20**
Perlhuhn, Scharlachs
andere höhere Vögel
Rund

Scoring and folding of
a 350gsm card.

Folding

As soon as you have more than two pages (greetings card with two panels, prospectus, folder, book cover, etc.), **finishing also involves folding, or even scoring**, because over and above 200gsm, paper becomes too rigid to pass through a folding machine and needs to be made more flexible or its fibres broken before it is folded. The same applies to plastic substrates. In this case, an impression has to be made at the folding point before the folding operation can take place.

It would be a mistake to add bleed to the side of a page where the fold will be. Any printed matter that is not a single leaf is considered to be a sequence of four-page signatures, even though most signatures are generally thicker than that: 8 pages (rarely), 12, 16, 24, or even 32 or more pages per signature. The pagination of a signature is limited only by the thickness of the paper used.

Possible folds according to paper type

Grammage	Number of folds per type of paper		
	Uncoated	**Coated**	**High Bulk Matt Art Coated**
250gsm*	4	8	4 (scoring)
200gsm	8	8	8
170gsm	16	16	16
140–150gsm	16	24	16
130–135gsm		24	24
120gsm	24		
115gsm		32	24/32
100gsm	32	32	32
90gsm	32	48	32
80gsm	32	48	48
70gsm	48	64	48

* From 250gsm, the paper must be scored.

The block

Folding operations create signatures. **If there are two or more signatures, they need to be collated to be sewn, glued, or stitched together to form a block, on which a cover is affixed.**

We have a series of numbered double pages that are ready for the next stage after each sheet has been folded into one or more signatures. Although your double-page spreads might all look alike on a flatplan, bear in mind that in reality **only the 'real' double-page spreads – the ones that are placed in their entirety on the printed sheet during the imposition phase – can really reproduce what you see on a computer screen.** In order to see two full pages that end up side by side as a result of folding the sheet, you can request a 'final imposition' from the printer. This has several consequences:

– **Aligning during printing:** this is something that any good press operator should keep an eye out for to ensure that the two halves of a double page that are not on the same ink zone are correctly lined up (see pages 197 and 199).

Examples of false double-page spreads correctly aligned.

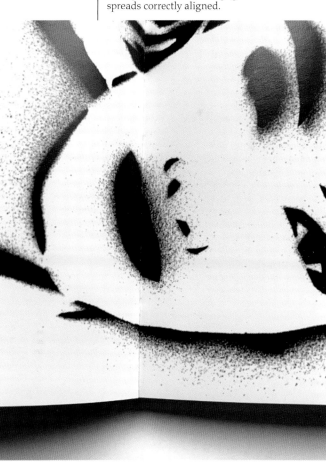

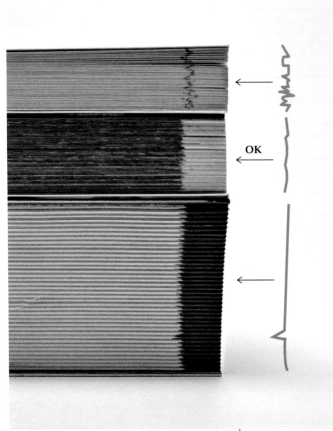

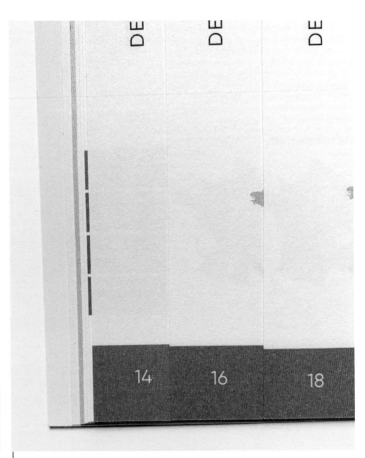

OK

Top, incorrect alignment due to
paper thickness; bottom, a
folding defect on a signature.

Vertical shift of a
coloured strip.

The correct distance between
a folio and the trim.

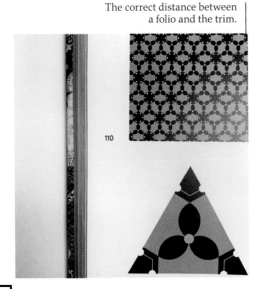

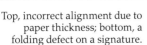

– **Aligning during the finishing phase:** folding and assembly of the
signatures also requires special care to avoid possible shift. Badly
aligned images can occur either because the folding machine is not
set correctly, the paper is too thick, or the signature has too many
pages and a discrepancy known as 'creep' occurs between the inner
and outer edge of the signature, as well as between the top and
bottom. This explains why it is difficult to get coloured sections to
align perfectly.

– **Organizing your graphic elements correctly:** this depends on you
and you alone. The elements must be arranged appropriately so
your plans aren't ruined by the technical constraints of the finishing
operations. Bear in mind that, most of the time, the line representing
the fold is actually a virtual line that is invisible on the screen but
will be visible, and possibly even in the way, once it becomes real. You

should therefore avoid putting a CEO's photo, a film star's nose, or even a price, a catalogue reference or text in the middle of a double-page spread; all or part of these elements risk disappearing into the gutter.

Particular attention should be paid to frames, borders and folios when they are close to the trim: the standard rule is to position them at least 1 cm (⅜ in) from the trim. The smaller an element and the closer to the trim it is, the more its position is liable to shift and any irregularities to become noticeable after folding and trimming. If you position a border 4 to 5 mm (around 3/16 in) from the trim and the folding shifts by just 1 millimetre, which is always possible, the width of your border will vary from one page to another by up to a quarter of its size: this inevitably becomes noticeable.

Brochures

In digital printing and in multifunction office printer/photocopiers, leaves are assembled in a block. This is either held together with glue and a small piece of cloth placed on the spine, by plastic combs, or by Wire-o systems.

Offset presses, especially web ones, have to operate within the constraints of signatures as printed signatures are folded and ready for assembly.

Sheet-fed presses allow greater freedom in the pagination of the signatures and allow you to juggle with variations in pagination and paper mixes. Whatever the situation, the main types of finishing are as follows:

Nested signatures / Saddle-stitched spine

The signatures are nested inside one another. There may be a cover added; two or several staples are applied in the fold of this super-signature that is held open 'astride' a saddle-stitcher before being trimmed.
This type of finishing operation, generally used for free booklets and product catalogues, is suitable for low paginations on fairly thin paper (80 to 100gsm). However, a special effect can be achieved for prestige publications by sacrificing pagination in favour of paper grammage and bulk.

A tracing paper band glued together.

The maximum thickness of a saddle-stitched signature cannot exceed 6 mm (¼ in). To give an example, 120 pages with semi-matt 115gsm coated paper 0.85 bulk*, or 80 pages with a 150gsm uncoated, 1 bulk**, or 80 pages with matt coated 115gsm and a bulk of 1.3***, etc. If you wish to go beyond these limits because you are looking for a particular aesthetic effect – like the famous magazine *Égoïste* – you can dispense with the stitching and leave the signatures free, just nested. Ideally it should have a sealed band, and poly bagging per unit is essential to hold it together for distribution.

Stitched spine brochure.

CALCULATING BLOCK THICKNESS

This is a theoretical calculation that works for all types of finishing operations. It gives you an idea of the appearance of your object, but it is strongly recommended to ask your printer for the exact calculation. It is advisable to order a blank mock-up, known as a 'dummy', which is the only way you can get a true picture to check the dimensions and see how your object feels when you handle it.

To calculate the thickness of a signature or an entire block, divide the grammage of the paper by 1,000, multiply it by the bulk, then multiply again by half the number of pages:

* (115/1,000) × 0.85 × (120/2) equals 5.87 mm.

** (150/1,000) × 1 × (80/2) equals 6 mm.

*** (115/1,000) × 1.3 × (80/2) equals 5.98 mm.

BANANA SKIN

Inserting signatures into each other causes a horizontal shift of up to 2 or 3 mm ($\frac{1}{16}$ to $\frac{1}{8}$ in) in the layout. Printers have software that recalculates the imposition based on this shift to help solve these problems, but it is best to avoid coloured bands on the vertical edge in the layout, otherwise they may differ in width once folded and trimmed.

Above, a sewn block;
below, a glued spine.

Stacked signatures: flat or square spine

There are two ways to produce a brochure with a square spine:

– **Glued spine (perfect binding)**: the signatures are assembled and the spine is ground with metal milling blades, which shave a few millimetres off the spine of the folded signatures to allow the glue to penetrate. A cover is then affixed to the glued spine.

– **Sewn spine**: the signatures are assembled, then sewn together with a sewing machine using textile thread; a cover is then affixed to the sewn block on the binding line. This type of block is also used for hardcover books that go through a case-in line, as we will see later.

Remember that signatures are always closed before binding because they are created by folding the printed sheets. During the final phase of binding, after the cover has been affixed and the **hinges** (see pages 214 and 215) glued, the three-knife trimming machine trims the cover and the non-trimmed signatures on three sides, thus freeing the leaves.

BANANA SKIN

The procedure that grinds off 2 or 3 mm (¹⁄₁₆ to ¹⁄₈ in) in the middle of each double page is generally controlled by the printer using software that recalculates the imposition, but it is prudent to check with them beforehand.

SEWN SPINE WITH VISIBLE THREAD

For reasons that are now apparent, it's not possible to produce a glued square spine (perfect binding) without a cover, because it's the cover that holds the block together in the absence of stitches.

However, it is possible to produce a finished sewn block with visible thread (also known as an 'exposed spine'). You cannot achieve this by simply leaving the cover off a normal sewn block. The glue used in this case is a very specific kind, because it needs to stay transparent rather than turning white. You can then choose to either leave the cover off (although this weakens the exterior of the block if the paper is thin), or make a cover with two pieces of thicker cover card, manually glued onto the first and last pages. This is a very sophisticated type of finishing that only a few specialists are able to do. If you find one, you could allow yourself an extra flourish by using different coloured threads to decorate the spine.

If you always look at the page layout of your product on a flat screen without ever seeing and handling real objects, you may get some nasty surprises.

When the same image runs across the inside cover and the first or last page of the block (e.g., double-page adverts in a magazine), the middle part of the image may end up under the glued hinge. This problem can be avoided in prepress by duplicating around 6 mm of material on each page where the fold will be.

Before you decide on the format and the spine thickness (6 to 8 cm/2¼ to 3 in maximum) for your product, consult your service provider to find out the minimum and maximum dimensions possible for automated binding operations.

Whether it's ground or sewn, the block for a brochure gets its cover attached on the binding line. The cover is glued onto the spine and onto a vertical 6 to 7 mm (¼ in) strip on the first and last pages. A clamp then applies pressure to the glued areas to secure the whole; that's what we call **glued hinges**. (It is possible to have a brochure without glued hinges, but you will need to consult specialists.)

How to create the cover of a brochure with a square (flat) spine
The cover of a standard brochure is the same size as its inner block. However, for a brochure with a spine you need to know the thickness of the spine to organize your prepress file. Once you've obtained this information from your printer, you just need to allow for a 5 mm (³⁄₁₆ in) trim around the cover when it's flat, and ditto for the interior pages. If, however, you've planned flaps, you will have a slight overflow between the block and the fold of the two flaps. In this case, ask the printer for a cover template so you can precisely position your graphic elements. It is advisable to allow an extra 2 to 3mm (¹⁄₁₆ to ⅛ in) for the fold of the flap.

SEWN OR GLUED?

A sewn spine is not always more solid than a glued spine. Yes, sewing is designed to ensure flexibility of opening and solidity of the block over time, and this is certainly the case for paper that weighs over 130gsm, especially if it's coated, because glue can rip off the surface mineral coating. However, porous uncoated papers 'fuse' with the glue; therefore perfect binding is particularly effective with thick paper.

A block's solidity usually has less to do with sewing and more with the quality of the glue used. All glues dry out and crack to some degree over time, except for PUR adhesive, which guarantees similar elasticity and solidity to sewing. If your spine is thin and your cover card not particularly thick, perfect binding is the best option; it is neater because of the absence of stitches.

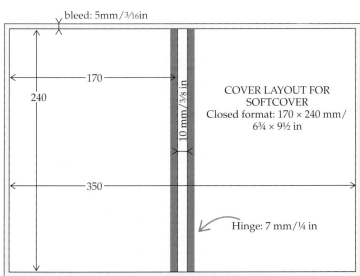

Sewn spine brochure,
cover with full flaps.

The flap must be shorter
than the cover board.

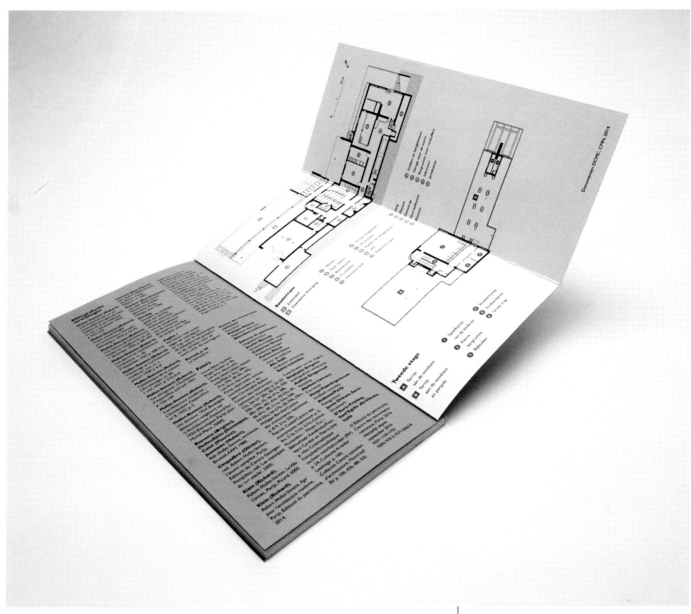

A tourist guide with a floor plan on one of the inside flaps. Note that it's only possible to have one flap on a cover.

Sewn or not, a brochure generally comes with a printed (or not) cover on paper, card or a specific, non-rigid material of variable grammage, which rarely exceeds 350gsm.

A cover can be plain or with flaps and the latter can vary in size. However, full flaps, designed to double the surface area of the cover boards, must be at least 1 cm shorter than the boards, because of the hinges that take up 7 mm (¼ in).

The flaps can have a structural function to make the cover firmer, or be used to provide information that remains immediately accessible (such as in a travel guide), or they can be purely aesthetic with highly imaginative variations.

The two flaps can differ.
The first folds outwards
and the second inwards.

Different die-cut shapes
superimposed between
the cover and the flap.

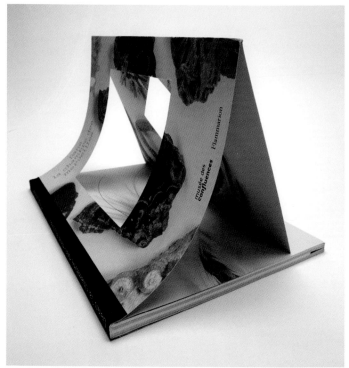

We'll see later that it's easy to affix cloth (or other material) to the spine of a rigid cover. However, on a brochure this is a fully manual operation, which involves a certain margin of error and a cost you need to be aware of.

On the binding line, either a cover with flaps is applied in several passes (trim fore edge of block, apply cover, trim head and tail), or a suitably equipped machine opens the already glued cover boards, trims the fore edge and then trims the head and tail.

It is possible to affix a **double cover** to a brochure that is either the same size or smaller than the latter.
Beware of the many technical traps lying in wait for you: the nature of the materials to be assembled, their rigidity and the type of glue can all cause things to go wrong if you don't take sufficient advice from your service provider.

A smaller overlay cover with different paper.

Two rigid cards that are coming apart.

Possible variations in a block

On an assembly line, a system of blades and suction cups opens the signature in the middle so that sewing operations can be performed and foldouts, etc. can be inserted. Understanding the mechanics of this helps you to know what can be automated and what can only be done as a manual or semi-manual operation. These criteria apply equally to a brochure or a hardcover book, because we are talking about the block and not the binding.

What can be done using automation?

– **Alternate signatures of different paper stocks**. The flatplan would need to take into account the paper variations.
– **Insert two-page dividers**: in reality, what happens each time is that a four-page signature is wrapped around a larger signature of 8, 12, 16 pages and so on. A leaf therefore appears at regular intervals, but that imposes some constraints on the flatplan.
– **Insert a four-page signature or a foldout**. This can be done as long as it is at the start of a signature, because the four pages will be held in place by a line of glue on the first or the last page of the signature concerned.

A series of signatures with different paper stocks.

- **Insert a four-page signature in the middle of a bigger signature**. The base of the signature and the base of the insert must be identical.
- **Insert one or several signatures into a block that are smaller than the main block**. This is only possible if the small signatures are placed at the beginning or the end of a large signature and in the following cases:
  - base smaller than that of the block: yes, as long as it is in line with the base of the block;
  - height less than that of the block: yes, as long as it is in line with the base of the block;
  - base and height less: no, but you can have them glued by hand at great expense.

BANANA SKIN

We have seen that the panel of a foldout must be shorter than the page it pulls out from (page 119). When a foldout is inserted into a block, the whole signature has to be shortened in relation to the rest of the block, as the trimming machine that trims the block may cut the foldout at the fold if it is flush with the fore edge of the block.

Also keep an eye on the following point: the three-knife trimming machine could run out of control if there is a large void and the machine has to deal with too many foldouts with empty spaces building up. This kind of empty space can also be an aesthetic issue. In addition, the external knife is jolted and the edge can tear and become ragged. In any case, **you need to know the imposition and folding planned by your printer** in order to know where you can insert a leaf or a signature, so you can accurately draw up your flatplan based on this information.

Three blocks with a signature that is shorter on the base. Bottom: the small signature is very thin and so invisible from the outside; middle: the gap is noticeable; top: the small signature is very thick, creating an imbalance in the block.

JAPANESE (OR CHINESE) FOLDING

Nowadays, it is possible to produce a simplified industrial version of this ancient Asian binding system. After printing, a sheet is slit into parallel strips and folded like an accordion. It is impossible to sew signatures folded in this way, as they cannot be opened with blades and suction cups. They are therefore assembled for perfect binding: the block is ground and the cover glued inline.

You can change the colour of the thread to give your object a more subtle and balanced finish.

Binding

The Chinese and Japanese traditionally opted for flexibility by using thin paper printed on a single side and assembled in four-page signatures, with the fold on the outer (fore) edge; the assembled block was held together with cord threaded through perforations. In the West, we have made the system more cost-effective by printing on both sides of the sheets, opening the signatures on the fore edge and assembling them with a more or less rigid system, i.e., the cover.

The sewn block, trimmed on three sides, is assembled on the case-in line with the other elements:

– **Two endpapers** laid out in an L-shape on both sides of the block, glued on the inside of the boards and along a 7 mm strip that attaches them to the first and last page of the block.

– **The cover** is laid flat on top of the spine of the block; gauze, or mull, is glued to the spine, sometimes with head and tail bands* and one or several ribbon markers. A mechanism re-folds the two cover boards and 'presses' it where the two glued strips are, tightening it all together on the two gutters (the equivalent of hinges in a brochure).

*Head and tail bands can be put on a spine of a minimum of 5 mm, no less; there are none on comics or children's books with a low pagination.

A ribbon marker.

Contemporary bindings inspired by old Asian designs.

A tail band.

The block is attached to the case (hardback cover) by the endpapers.

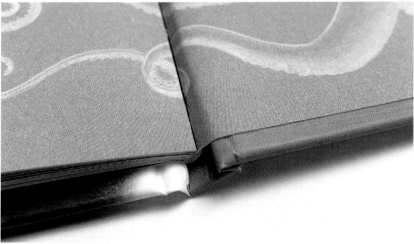

'In text' endpapers or 'self-ends'.

ENDPAPERS

Endpapers are essential for putting a block and a cased (hardback) cover together. They are usually made of fairly thick and flexible paper: 120 to 150gsm uncoated, depending on the solidity required. They can be blank (not printed), produced with mass-dyed speciality paper, or printed in one or several colours. The endpapers can also be 'in text' or 'self ends', i.e., the first page of the first signature and the last page of the last signature are glued to the two cover boards: these two leaves will therefore form the structure of the endpapers.

Cover of a hardback
book with a printed and
laminated board, cloth
on the spine and two
pastels hot stamped for
the title.

How to optimize all the parameters of a
very thick book:
– 2 cover boards of 283 mm (11⅛ in)
– 2 turn-ins of 15 mm (⁹⁄₁₆ in)
– 2 bleeds of 5 mm (³⁄₁₆ in)
– 2 boards of 3 mm (⅛)
=
306 mm (12¹⁄₁₆ in)
for each cover board
There are 2 boards so
=
612 mm (24¹⁄₁₆ in) +
spine thickness 63 mm (2½ in)
=
675 mm (26½ in)

It is possible to place three covers on a
70 × 100 cm/27½ × 39½ in machine
(see diagram).

Case-in lines process maximum and minimum formats in an automated system, beyond which you need to switch to semi-manual, or manual. The maximum dimensions depend on the equipment a particular bindery has. As a general rule, you can achieve 27.5 × 34 cm (10¾ × 13½ in) or 29.5 × 36 cm (11½ × 14 in) automated, and 30 × 38 cm (12 × 15 in) in semi-manual; for a horizontal format, the base can be a maximum of 29 or 30 cm (11½ or 12 in) with a fairly variable height.

A production line can fit a cover on a block of a maximum thickness of 7 or 8 cm (2¾ or 3 in). Several factors come into play when choosing a format: if you have a very wide spine, you need to ensure that when you add together the spine board or piece, the thickness of the board and the turnover, they will fit onto a plate.

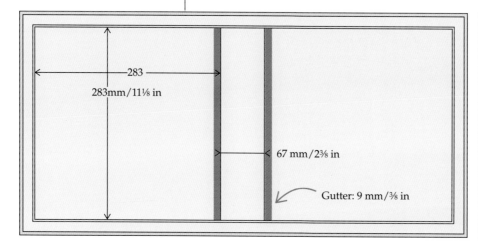

283
283mm/11⅛ in

67 mm/2⅜ in

Gutter: 9 mm/⅜ in

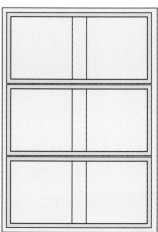

What are the main types of binding?

There are three types:

Hardcover or case binding. On a case-in line, the block is attached via the endpapers to a cover usually composed of three pieces of board (two cover boards and the spine) on which a sheet of paper is glued, with a 15-mm (½ in) strip all around. The endpapers are then glued to the inside cover of the cover boards and the edge of the cover paper.

The distance between the block and the board is called the overflow; it is generally between 3 and 5 mm (³⁄₁₆ in), but this can be reduced to 1 mm to produce narrower objects that look like something halfway between a paperback and a hardback.

The board is between 1.5 and 4 mm (¹⁄₁₆ to ³⁄₁₆ in) thick. Technically, there is no relationship between a block and the thickness of the board, so you can make a very thick block with small, thin board or, conversely, a low pagination and very thick cover boards.

Minimal board overflow on the top book; classic overflow on the bottom book.

The mass-dyed black board extends the aesthetic effect of the cut-out on a cover printed on a black background.

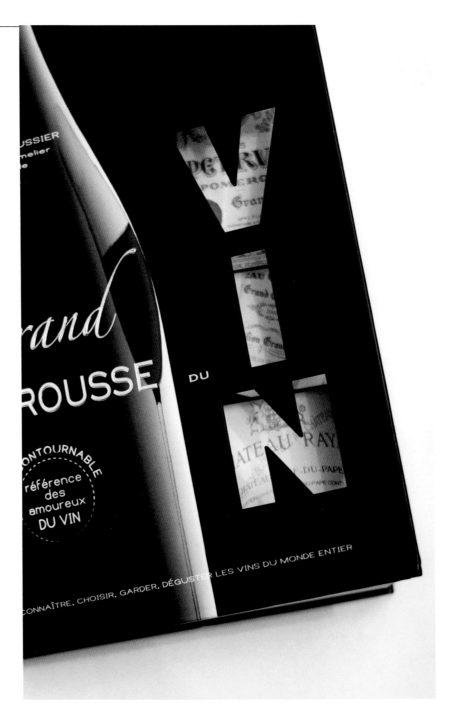

A hardcover can have a flat or a rounded spine.

The only technical limitation is the total thickness of the spine, which cannot be less than 3 mm if it is to be put through the case-in line. (There are specific production lines for small spines like the ones on a comic.) The board is usually grey because it is intended to be covered in paper or another material. However, there are mass-dyed versions, which are extremely sophisticated when it comes to creating specific effects, but are costly and not commonly used.

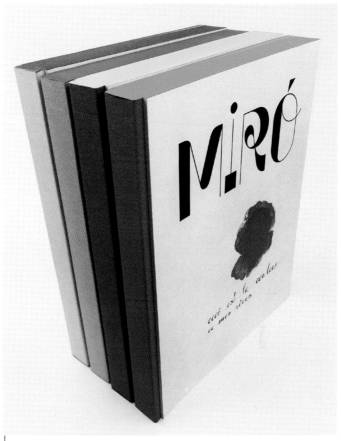

Flexibinding. | | Bodoni binding.

Flexibound. The process is the same, but instead of paper glued on board, flexible card is used and the 15 mm edges of the cover are folded in behind the endpapers before they are glued on. This type of binding works well for objects that need to be flexible and open well, such as guidebooks and rulebooks.

For the cover, you can opt for semi-rigid 300 to 350gsm card that you would use for an ordinary brochure, but with this type of finishing 'wrinkles' frequently occur the first few times the book is opened. The best material is a 300gsm glossy coated paper that will remain sufficiently flexible to prevent this defect.

The spine of a flexibound book is always slightly rounded due to the suppleness of the material used for the cover.

Bodoni binding. Cloth is applied around the spine of a sewn block, followed by endpapers along with two cover boards, with or without cover material. These operations are partially or totally manual and therefore expensive, depending on the binding tools used.

✳ TIP

One popular option is to leave raw edges on two or three sides. This gives a hardcover book a Bodoni appearance at an affordable price. Be aware, though, that a cover produced in this way is more fragile at the corners as the cover material tends to come unstuck and the board loses its rigidity. Some people opt for a two-sided cut, just at the head and tail. Pay attention to one particular detail, however: it's not just a matter of putting a hardcover or an ordinary flexibound work through the trimmer; the 15 mm of overflow must stay flat when the cover is assembled before casing-in, otherwise it will be visible under the endpapers after trimming. Make sure your supplier knows how to handle this option (below).

✳ TIP

You can have raw edges with flexibinding and produce a kind of softcover with endpapers and an articulated spine, which can be interesting for certain objects (see right).

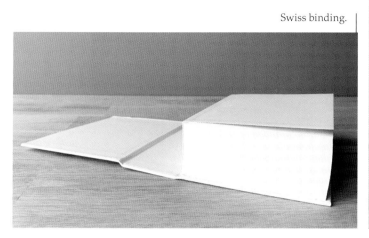

Leporello.

Swiss binding.

What are the other types of binding?

For **Swiss binding**, the standard hardback cover has a single endpaper across the entire interior. The block is held together by a cloth on the spine and the last page is glued onto the back inside board either directly or by means of an endpaper.

A **leporello binding** consists of pages folded accordion- or concertina-style in a single strip or as several strips glued one after the other. The first page of the folded object is sometimes glued onto a cover board of semi-rigid card.

Wire-o or spiral binding. A block of signatures trimmed on all four sides is perforated and assembled using wire loops.

Wire-o binding.

Singer sewn.

Moleskine-style.

Singer-sewn binding uses the same sewing technique as for textiles, and is done on a specific machine that sews either a large signature open in the middle or a closed block on the board 3 or 4 cm (1¼ or 1½ in) from the spine. These are generally manual operations.

Moleskine-style binding is a system used to place a particular material – paper, imitation leather or fabric – on a very thin board padded on the corners that have previously been cut to make them rounded.

Which hardcover should you choose?

A hardback book cover generally consists of three board sections: two cover boards and a spine to which a particular material is glued. This is most often 135gsm coated paper, printed and laminated. It is essential to laminate this type of paper otherwise it will quickly become damaged, especially on the corners.

Cover boards can be decorated in many different ways: real or imitation cloth, leather or imitation leather, as well as other materials that are flexible enough to be wrapped around the board without cracking at the fold or on the gutters.

A cover board can also be paired with foam of varying thicknesses. The materials used to cover boards are specially designed for binding to ensure they have enough elasticity to fulfil their function. It is not advisable to use uncoated paper on a cover; opt for materials such as Wibalin, Geltex and others that imitate uncoated stock but are suitable for cover material. There are extensive catalogues of these kinds of materials in different brands with different colours and embossing as well as neutral versions designed for four-colour printing.

Foam board.

Industrial fabric colour swatch.

BANANA SKIN

You can't stick the fabric or leather of your choice directly on a board; you need to perform what's called a 'backing' process. This means the material needs to be glued with a special glue onto the appropriate sheet of paper before the whole thing is glued to the board with a special binding glue. Unless you have a massive budget, it's better to choose binding materials from catalogues, which are already fairly expensive.

Asymmetrical cloth spine.

A combination of two materials can used for the same cover: paper for the boards and cloth (imitation cloth or leather, etc.) for the spine. This type of binding is generally called 'quarter binding'. The second material can be placed asymmetrically around the spine, more on one cover board than the other.

Alternatively, the spine can be covered in cloth and the two cover boards can stay untreated and embellished with a variety of graphic effects: dry stamping, hot stamping, varnishing and silk-screen colours.

CENTRING A COVER

Depending on whether a book is a paperback or a hardback, the graphic elements are not centred on the cover boards in the same way. More importantly, they are almost never centred in relation to the width of the boards.

On a softcover, the cover boards are 7 mm (¼ in) wider due to the hinge; on a hardcover, there is 1 cm (³⁄₈ in) of board and gutter between the spine and the board. Logic would dictate that you centre a title in relation to the actual cover board, whereas on a screen you might instinctively centre it in relation to the total width including the joint and gutter. In fact, centring a title is an art in itself. Depending on the elements involved, you have to create an optical illusion: geometric shapes, a frame or the size of the title will sometimes cause you to move a few millimetres to one side or the other.

✳ TIP
Which direction should the text on the spine of a book or magazine face? In the English-speaking world and elsewhere, you tilt your head towards the right to read, whereas in Europe and Latin America they do the opposite.

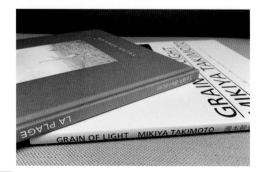

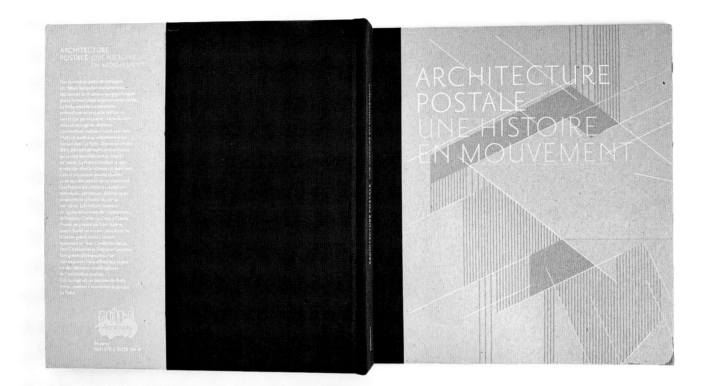

Cover with cloth spine on untreated board with cold stamping and three silk-screen printing processes: one varnish and two pastels.

How to prepare the cover file for a hardback book

Only the printer can provide a cover plotter with the exact dimensions of each element. You can also ask for a blank dummy and do the measurements yourself, but it's better to have a file to work from.

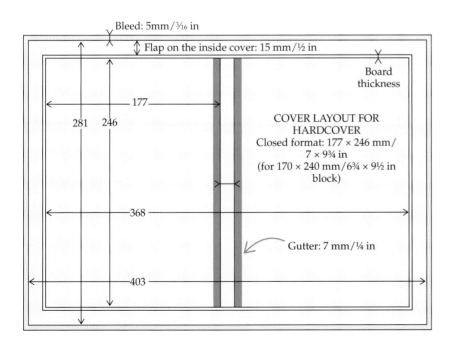

Bleed: 5mm/³⁄₁₆ in

Flap on the inside cover: 15 mm/½ in

Board thickness

177

281   246

COVER LAYOUT FOR HARDCOVER
Closed format: 177 × 246 mm/
7 × 9¾ in
(for 170 × 240 mm/6¾ × 9½ in block)

368

Gutter: 7 mm/¼ in

403

BANANA SKIN

While 5 mm (³⁄₁₆ in) of trim is sufficient for a softcover, 15 mm (¹⁄₂ in) is essential for a hardcover to ensure that the endpapers and the return on the inside of the cover are properly superimposed. Don't forget this detail when you're preparing a file for a hardcover.

Covers being laminated (matt).

Cover finish

The cover is a vital part of a publication that justifies extra creativity and budget.

There are several technical options.
- **Inline protective varnish**: used on cloth, imitation cloth or cover material printed in offset, to strengthen the ink and protect against dirt.
- **Lamination** (matt, satin, gloss, soft touch, anti-scratch): protects the printed matter while giving it an extra dimension. It protects better than a simple varnish and is applied to the entire printed sheet by machines that apply a film the same width as the sheet.

Be aware that if you apply a laminate over a metallic spot colour (gold, bronze, etc.), the gloss of the inks is largely neutralized by the film, especially if it is matt. Why not spend a little more and go for a hot foil stamp? **Laminating changes the way paper absorbs light and reflects colours. Printed colours can look very different depending on whether you apply matt or gloss laminate.** Some repro specialists can plan for this colour shift and show you proofs simulating different laminates on different papers; it's worth spending the money for this extra peace of mind.

Foreground: Pantone metal plus lamination. Background: matt lamination plus metallic hot stamping.

Dry stamping (debossing) plus matt hot stamping.

- **Offset 'spot' varnish**: a non-pigmented, water- or oil-based ink that behaves like a primary colour or a Pantone, which is used for dot-on-dot inline varnishing of very small details (see pages 99 and 192). This is not to be confused with 'spot', commonly known as 'selective' varnish, which is a silk-screen printing technique (see page 190).
- **UV varnish**: you can use silk-screen techniques on a sheet previously printed in offset to rework specific details or larger or smaller areas on the sheet up to and including the whole sheet (see page 104). There are different types of varnish: granular, canvas, glitter, mirror (not to be confused with 'mirror paper'), and relief, which creates a raised effect (see page 105) and exists in many colours that you can choose from screen printers' colour charts.
- **Embossing/debossing (dry stamping)**: is a metal stamp that exerts pressure on the board, covered or not, and leaves a visible trace – text or a pattern (see page 107). *Embossing* creates raised relief and *debossing* creates cavities. In the latter case, two plates (clichés), one male and one female, are required to exert pressure on both sides of the board. This operation is mainly designed for hardback covers, as the thickness of the board makes the cavity or the relief more visible. However, it is possible to deboss or emboss semi-rigid card, with a less visible but sometimes interesting effect. A dry stamp can also be used to create a debossed panel in which a label printed on special (self-adhesive) paper can be stuck (known as a 'tip in').

✳ TIP
You've printed your cover and you're not sure which laminate to use. Sticking a strip of shiny sticky tape and a strip of matt sticky tape, the kind you can reposition, on the printed sheet will give you a fairly good idea of the final result.

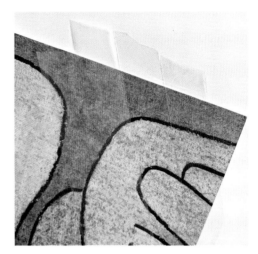

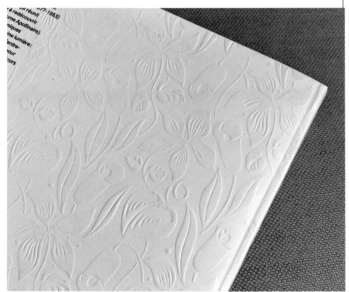

Dry stamping in relief (embossing) on the entire surface of a flexibound cover.

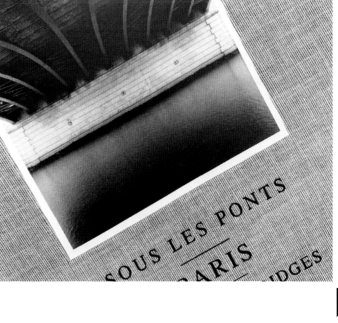

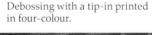

Debossing with a tip-in printed in four-colour.

Opposite: Metallic foils chart for hot stamping. Left: silver foil stamp.

– **Hot stamping (foil blocking)**: this is the same operation as imprinting a depression, but with the addition of a foil or pastel. It is generally used for titles and borders, but can also be used for larger surfaces with graphic and typographic elements.

The classic foils are gold, silver or other metallic colours. These materials have perfect coverage and are relatively solid. A wide range of non-metallic colours is also available, though pastels, both glossy and matt, have much less coverage and are more fragile. Transparency can be controlled by printing behind the area in a colour similar to that of the chosen foil. Ask for advice if you want to print on larger surfaces.

The finish known as flocking, in which short fibres are applied to a glue-coated surface using an electromagnetic process, produces an appearance similar to suede, velvet or wool.

Die cutting can be used for a soft or hard cover. A tool is made in the shape of the surface to be cut out, based on the same principle as that used for embossing. Laser cutting can be used to obtain high-precision patterns.

Any additional elements on a cover after offset printing (laminate, varnishes, silk-screen printing and hot stamps) are applied to a whole sheet. This is the case for a basic invitation card, a book jacket, a belly band, or a sticker as well as for the cover of a paperback book. Several copies of the object are printed on the same sheet at the same time and the second pass is done on a form whose individual elements are subsequently cut out. There is one exception: a hot or dry stamp on the cover of a bound work is applied on individual covers, once the material – paper, cloth, imitation cloth, which might be printed, laminated or screen printed – has been glued onto the board. In this case, striking the image is easy and clean, as it leaves its mark in the thickness of the underlying board.

Cut-out on coloured card
previously printed in black.

The cost of a dry or hot stamp
includes the manufacture of a tool,
so the price will depend on the size
and the quantity of foil required.
The surface area is calculated as
a percentage of the space occupied
across the plate. A large title on the
cover will cost you a lot less than a
few tiny details spread out over the
whole cover. When in a quote you see
'hot stamp 25% coverage', this means
that only a quarter of the overall
area of the plate will be stamped. If
you want details spread everywhere,
you should specify **100%** of the
surface in your request or, better
still, send the printer a **PDF** of your
project so they can calculate their
quote more accurately.

PREPARING A FILE FOR HOT STAMPING, DRY STAMPING, SCREEN PRINTING OR DIE CUTTING

Only the elements that can be printed in offset should appear in your basic file: the four basic colours and any spot colours or inline varnishes. Any additional element that uses another technique (screen printing, stamping, cutting, etc.) should be in a separate file. Even if you gather together all the graphic elements to visualize the whole and produce a proof, it is essential to have a clearly identified independent layer that is set up as any solid colour. There is no need to specify or try to recreate the colour of the foil in the file; just specify the foil reference on your printer PO. Don't make the mistake of putting everything together in one file.

You need to supply a specific file if you want to make a gift holder, a folder with flaps, a cover for a presentation box or an unusual cover that needs die cutting. As with the stamps and varnishes, on the first layer you'll have the four-colour or Pantone base, on the second layer, the vector drawing of the layout that shows the borders of the finished object, and on the third, the additional graphic elements. Your service provider will supply you with the exact measurements to use on your file.

Die cutting file.

+

Hot stamping file.

=

Foil blocking on coloured paper.

Other types of finishes

Edge decoration was originally used to stop dust from getting into books thanks to a very thin gold leaf applied to the edges, which still allowed the pages to come apart. Wealthy people had all three edges of the block gilded; those who were not so well off just the top one.

Since the sixteenth century, many edges have been red or marbled. This adornment, like gilding, served to embellish and protect books that were designed to be handled a lot, such as those used for church services.

Nowadays, we can play around with this decorative effect (which has a cost implication) to obtain very different effects, including laser printing of images or patterns. Bear in mind when planning your schedule: for a brochure or a bound book with cut flush edges, i.e., with the grey board showing, edging is applied to the finished object once the cover has been affixed; for a standard hardcover book, edging is applied to the sewn block before casing.

Decorative edging often takes a good week in specialized workshops and involves extra shipping to and from your printers.

Ideally, the same colour should be used for the cover and the coloured edge. Dark-coloured edging on a light cover may soil a paperback or a bound book with raw edges. This problem doesn't arise with a hardcover book, as the block is edged before finishing.

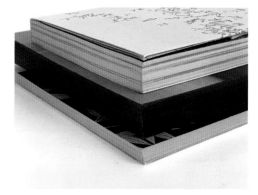

Dividers.

Rounded corners. Top, a book entirely in board that has been die cut, while the two others have been ground.

You can have specialists do **thumb indexes or dividers** on a finished block. These can be round, rectangular or square. It is important to ask your service provider about the rules for positioning graphic elements around the thumb indexes. As with edging, allow a few extra days in your schedule.

Once your product is finished, you can still add a variety of nice little extras, such as rounded corners on a brochure. This is done with a special tool that planes the corners of a block to make them rounded. This can only be done on a flexible block.

On a rigid volume, only rather expensive die cutting can achieve the same effect. This is the case for some children's books produced using the complex board book technique that we won't go into here (you need to contact specialists in this type of finishing, as many varieties of materials can be used).

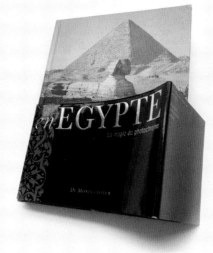
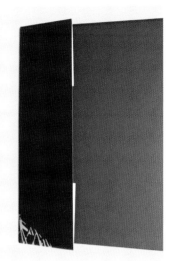

Jacket, half-jacket, jacket
with French folds.

Belly bands.

Other accessories

A book or brochure cover can have a dust jacket: a standard jacket with flaps, a half-jacket, or even French folds for heavy and luxurious books.

The horizontal or vertical belly band can be positioned in various ways. In some cases, this is done manually.

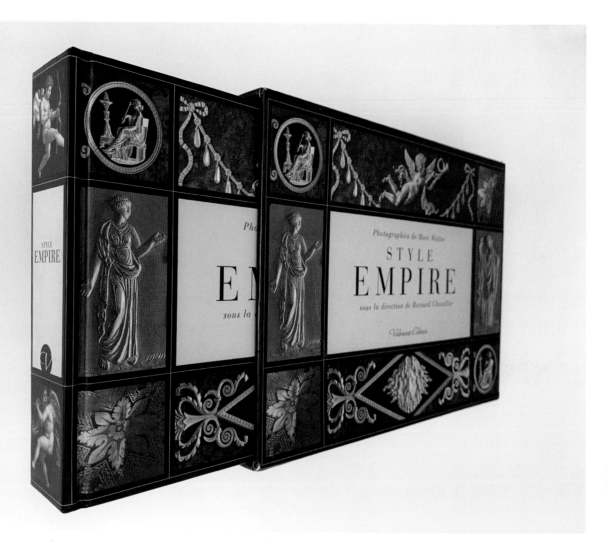

✤ TIP
You are preparing a publication that combines a hardcover book with a softcover booklet in a presentation box. Ask for the layout for the cover of the bound book and work out the dimensions of the accompanying booklet based on the size of the external board, so the two objects end up being the same size and format.

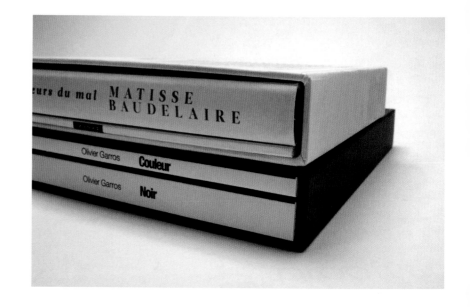

Here are a few examples of different types of slipcases and presentation boxes:

– Dust protection slipcase, printed or not

Materials used: speciality card, possibly varnished, or 250, 300 or 350gsm card coated on one side and laminated. They can be offset or screen printed in the same way as brochure covers.

– Presentation box

Materials used: 2 to 4 mm (¹⁄₁₆ to ³⁄₁₆ in) board, covered with laminated paper or cover material, as for covers. You can add hot stamping, dry stamping, screen printing, etc., as well as cloth head and tail bands.

Cases and presentation boxes can be manufactured industrially if they fall within the maximum formats that your service providers handle. It is essential to ask them for a layout so you can do the graphic design correctly, including bleeds and turn-ins.

– Telescope box, clamshell-style box (slipcases)

These are essentially manual creations that require a little research into suitable service providers and careful price studies.

⚠ *Be careful with the different layouts of a slipcase or presentation box: counter-intuitively, board 1 is the opposite way round from the cover board. Here is how you should position your titles:*

BOOK

Back cover	Front cover (board 1)

PRESENTATION BOX

Front cover (board 1)	Back cover

 Telescope box. Clamshell box.

> ✱ TIP
> **If the material on which you are going to print the barcode does not guarantee readability (textured paper, cloth, imitation cloth, etc.), a self-adhesive label printed in black and white is sometimes unavoidable.**
> **If you are really unsure, have the code printed inside the book too – on the colophon, for example.**

BARCODES

Your book or catalogue is truly beautiful, but if the barcode is missing or wrong, it will remain in the box and not be distributed. Graphic designers would rather dispense with them; they all dream of finding a way to alter these unsightly, space-consuming features to suit their aesthetic criteria; we would love them to be coloured, printed in negative on a coloured background, screen printed on mass-dyed material in a wide variety of textures… A barcode, like a QR code, is a line image that needs to be machine-readable by scanners. It is based on standardized criteria for the nature and purpose of your product. You can find these criteria online. For offset printing, use a 100% black or very dark colour. Composite shades are not permitted, as the smallest detection problem – which is inevitable in thin bars although invisible to the naked eye – compromises readability.

–A code must be accessible and the correct size according to the relevant standard;

– The bars must be a minimum height and surrounded by 'quiet zones' (at least five times wider than the thinnest bar) so the scanner can determine where the reading zone starts and ends;

– The code must be printed in high contrast – black on white being the ideal;

– It's best to run a test with a scanner (or ask your printer). White lines on a very dark background can be readable, especially if you're printing on highly reflective materials such as metal; film and lacquered cardboard do not respond well to infrared.

While laser impression and thermal transfer printing produce accurate printing on all kinds of surfaces, in gravure or offset printing, the barcode can only be read if the image is sharp and the texture of the printed substrate is smooth.

FAILURES AND FIXES

The scanner does not recognize your barcode or an incorrect price has been printed in the code, which is now unusable: have an adhesive label printed and stick it on.

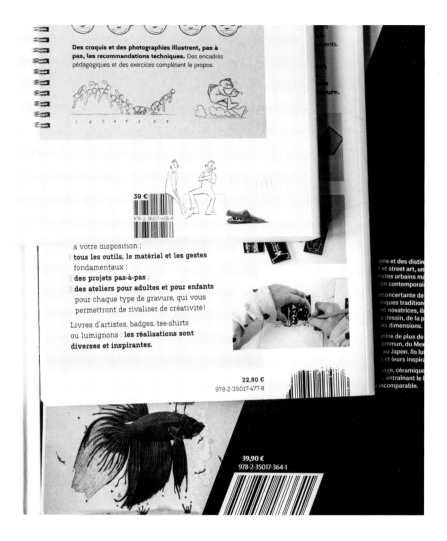

Why does a hardcover cost more than a softcover?

The binding process involves more complex operations and more expensive materials. Until you get to the sewn block, everything is the same; but for a rigid cover to stay on a block, you have to add endpapers (possibly printed) and material – board, cover materials, possibly laminated – all of which are much more expensive than basic semi-rigid card. As you can't really ask the printer to charge the same price, it's up to you to decide what you want to achieve with your object. If it is a book that is going to be sold, you'll need to adapt the sales price; a hardback sells for more than a paperback.

Checklist
COORDINATE THE FINISHING

- **Plan for trim and bleed for full-page images.**
- **Keep sensitive elements away from the trim (folio, borders, frames).**
- **Check the imposition: number of pages per signature.**
- **Think about the alignment of images in double-page spreads, and be careful with the cover/block alignment of brochures.**
- **Adjust the size of flaps and foldouts.**
- **Request a layout for a cover, a presentation box or die-cut shape.**
- **Ask for a blank mock-up/dummy.**
- **Check the white point of the interior paper and cover material to make sure colours look the same.**
- **Take care to separate the different elements when you are preparing the files: interior CMYK/Pantone/selective varnish – cover CMYK/Pantone + hot/dry stamp + screen printing.**

5

Packaging and shipping

You have created the perfect article (well, almost; complete perfection is unattainable): your flyer, annual report, artist's book, dictionary, poster or diary is a total success and everyone is delighted with the advance copies; you're on-time, just; you're going on holiday tomorrow, just before shipping, because you've worked really hard these past few weeks…

Here's how to enjoy that well-deserved holiday without stumbling at the final step, which could cost you your client's goodwill, your boss's respect and your spouse's forbearance.

It's simple: you just have to plan everything in advance, like you've done for your trip. Whether you're going skiing, on a beach holiday or halfway around the world, you book your travel and accommodation well in advance, right?

Packaging

This is often missing in many requests for quotes and it's a shame…
Every product that leaves a printer's must have a minimum amount of packaging so it can be shipped with some degree of protection.
Your business cards and flyers arrive in small boxes or in stacks wrapped in cellophane, but bigger products that cannot be handled manually require pallets so they can be loaded in a vehicle, sometimes stacked on top of each other. These pallets will be strapped and possibly wrapped in cellophane.

It's up to you to decide on the specific packaging for your articles.
– **Cellophane packaging**: this is usually a thick (high-density) and slightly translucent film that protects and separates the articles into piles.
– **Low-density unitary film**: thin transparent film designed to protect a single object.

- **Blister:** a transparent plastic used when you want to combine two or more products (a magazine and a small gift book or other product), or when you want to affix a label for a mailshot.
- **Cardboard boxes:** obligatory for some distributors, they are always advisable to facilitate stock handling, especially if the recipient is a company, institution or business where small quantities of printed matter must be easy to store and move.
- **Individual boxes:** corrugated cardboard packaging designed to protect very heavy, valuable or fragile items. Useful for postal delivery.

CAN PLASTIC FILM BE ENVIRONMENTALLY FRIENDLY?

There are plastic films made from starches or corn, designed to disintegrate when they come into contact with water, moisture or x-rays. While it is possible to use these to wrap objects, they are hard to use to wrap pallets in a printer's, where strength and durability are key.

However, there are polyethylene-based films that are recyclable, as they can be recovered, melted and transformed into granules.

TIP
When should you use single-unit plastic shrink-wrapping or poly bagging? When you want to protect the cover throughout its sales journey; when you want to protect the contents of a book or magazine that includes an additional inserted product (CD, booklet, sample, photo print, etc.); when you don't want customers to leaf through the product in a bookshop or a news stand.

Some products are sent by mail, and it's not unusual to have to assemble several objects, printed or not, to send in the same parcel. In this case, it's important to check with your service provider which formats and thicknesses they are able to handle, the total weight of the parcel based on postal rates and how files for personalizing the delivery will be managed. **You also need to give detailed instructions concerning any insertion (loose or in a specific place) of other objects, as well as for affixing labels or stickers.**

Don't make a final decision on the design of your printed object before you have considered the various parts of its journey through a printer's and elsewhere.

FAILURES AND FIXES

Is the shrink wrap protecting your publication poor-quality or defective? You can have the film removed and the object re-wrapped at a book doctor, where this can be done effectively for a reasonable price. This is also a good solution when you need to replace a defective jacket, adhesive labels and stickers, add a belly band, a blister pack, or any other operation that requires only basic tools.

Delivery

Well before your printing job is finished, give your printer all the necessary information: the table below is fairly exhaustive and you should try to complete all the details for each delivery point.

You might be delivering to a company, a private household or a storage facility. Each location has different delivery conditions that have a financial and logistical impact.

Distributors who specialize in newspapers or publishing have unloading bays for heavy goods vehicles and are equipped with pallet jacks. They also have specific opening hours: you often need to book a slot several days in advance, otherwise they might refuse to unload.

If you're delivering to a museum in a medieval castle, your carrier has the choice between a path that goes up some steps onto a cobbled street, or a wooden footbridge over a moat. In either case, you need to have the appropriate equipment and a van equipped with a pallet jack that can get as close to the entrance as possible. You then need to check that the on-site stores have the appropriate equipment and staff to take the catalogues inside.

Title of the work:

Contact person

Quantities	Company name	Contact name	Address	Telephone	Email	Opening hours	Equipment*	Comments

* specify whether it is a warehouse equipped for trucks (unloading bay), or whether you need to plan for a truck with a tail lift and pallet jack, plus the carrier to help unload.

Deliveries in a town or city centre are awkward and often complicated by traffic issues and the safety regulations specific to a given institution, so you have to be sure that a contact person is available to coordinate receipt of the delivery. It is essential that the carrier has the telephone number of the person in charge who will be there on the day of delivery.

When you send a delivery to your customer (or are expecting a delivery yourself), bear in mind that the main carrier hired by your printer will dispatch the contents of their large truck and entrust your pallet(s) to a freight forwarder, who in turn will pass your goods on to a second carrier with a smaller vehicle. Drivers can sometimes have navigation and even language issues. That's why everything needs to be clear, precise, and planned in advance to avoid leaving too many grey areas or last-minute queries. A delivery driver who arrives the day before a new library is officially opened and can't find the entrance causes mayhem…

All goods are delivered on one or more pallets. If specific prior instructions have not been given, the driver will simply unload the pallets and leave them on the side of the road or on the pavement: hence the importance of planning the logistics as well as the packaging so that the delivered goods can be moved fairly easily. If you need them to be left in a specific place (on a particular floor of a building, for example), you should specify this in advance and pay an extra handling charge.

Shipping abroad

It is important to know if your items are being delivered by truck or if you need to organize transport by boat, in which case **your goods will travel in containers, which could lead to humidity issues**. Don't forget that paper and cardboard are materials made of fibre and that temperature excursions, among other things, can cause trouble. When paper is delivered at the height of summer in Spain, the printer probably has air-conditioning in their factory and will wait a day or two before putting the paper through the press. Similarly, your Chinese printer has to take precautions when shipping by boat. Excessive haste is always a problem in production.

Shipping to certain countries may mean adhering to specific standards, such as fumigating the pallets.

BANANA SKIN

You should always check if the price given by your foreign printers is CIF (Cost Insurance and Freight) or FOB (Free on Board, which would otherwise be down to you to pay); if printing outside your own country or free trade region, you need to organize a freight forwarder, provide specific documents and pay customs duties. Be proactive and plan ahead to avoid a situation in which your goods are stuck in a port on the other side of the world.

Transport by air is very expensive (charged per kilo) and should only be used for a few advance copies or very lightweight, low-volume products.

Transport hazards

Minor accidents can occur during transport: over-enthusiastic braking can jostle the pallets in the truck and cause damage; a storm while transferring goods from a six-ton truck to a van could make the cardboard boxes wet. In most cases, everything will go smoothly because the pallets are properly packed and wrapped. If, however, a problem is noted on arrival, it is very important to take photos and leave a detailed comment on the carrier's delivery note. Without this, any subsequent claim will either be futile or conflictual at the very least.

We have come full circle and are back where we started: the importance of planning properly and paying attention to the details that will make your life easier.

No single detail is more important than another. The technical side and the logistical side contribute equally to a successful outcome, so I'll say it again: start at the end and all will be well!

Checklist

COORDINATE THE DELIVERY

Communicate packaging and delivery instructions, along with contact details, well in advance.

Plan the packaging according to the storage facility.

Organize customs formalities for work printed outside the destination country.

IMPOSITION AND FLATPLAN OF THIS BOOK

This book is composed of 264 pages numbered from 1 to 264, and 2 × 4 non-numbered endpapers, making a total of 272 pages obtained as follows*:

– **five sheets of 48 pages,** folded in 2 × 24 pages (except sheet 4: 24 + 16 pages), printed on a 120 × 160 machine, with 150gsm matt coated paper, bulk 1.01, in an optimized 129 × 110 format (following the direction of the fibres), as the total quantity allows this.

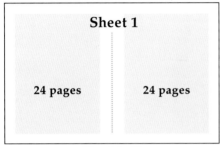

Page 1 to 48

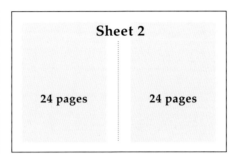

Page 81 to 128

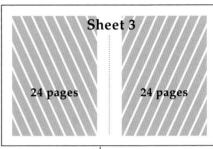

Page 129 to 152   Page 241 to 264

Half of sheet 3 is used after sheet 2, half at the end of the block; the aim was to insert sheet four, which is printed with an additional colour to illustrate the point about Pantone in the prepress chapter from page 162 to page 180.

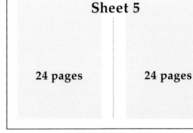

Page 153 to 192

Page 193 to 240

– **two sheets of 16 pages,** folded into 2 × 16 pages, printed on a 70 × 100 machine: sheet six in 150gsm glossy coated paper, and sheet seven in 140gsm uncoated. Both were printed on standard 64 × 88 'against the fibre' paper, due to the small quantity.

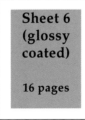

Page 49 to 64

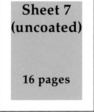

Page 65 to 80

– **The cover** was printed four-up on a 70 × 100 machine, on 135gsm gloss coated paper in standard 70 × 100 format.

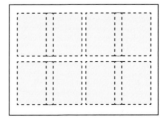

* The imposition diagrams shown on these pages refer to the printing of the original French edition of this book.

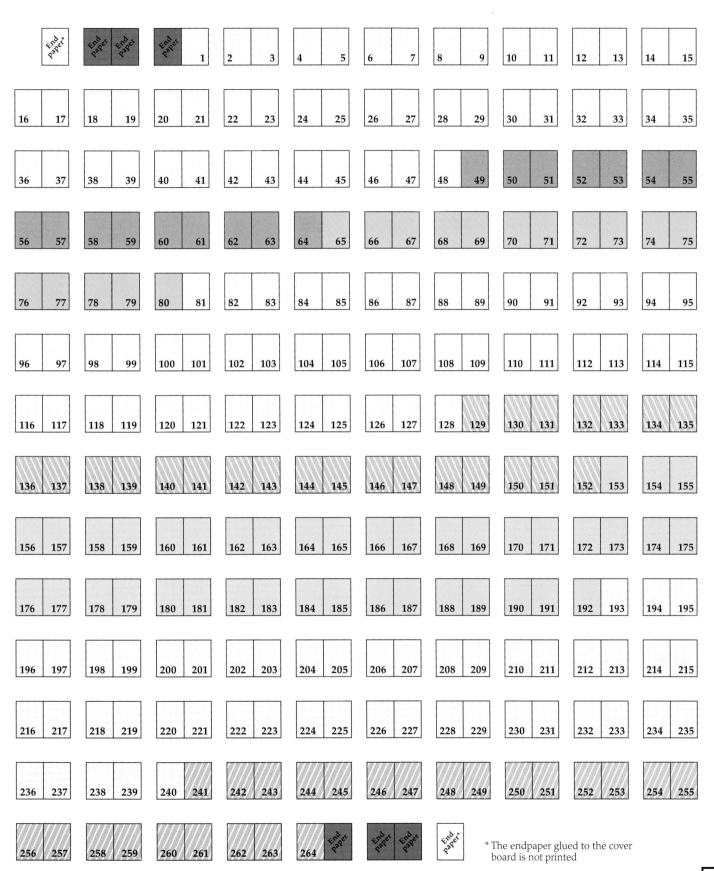

* The endpaper glued to the cover
  board is not printed

CONCLUSION

Production has been to my professional life what sewing has been to my leisure activities, because these two worlds are very similar: textures and materials, prints, sewing and cutting machines, not to mention the 'haberdashery/notions cupboard' that you open each time you choose colours and finishes to make a printed object beautiful.

Supervising the production of projects, be they huge or modest in scope, gives me the same pleasure as seeing a well-made garment without a crease.

You learn a lot by doing, by talking to others and often by making mistakes. Although perfection should be your goal, welcome the inevitable mistakes you make along the way and consider them as learning tools. Minor mistakes can be found in this book: they are mine or my colleagues' and they illustrate much better than a long explanation the pitfalls you learn to avoid over time.

I hope I have helped you to avoid the banana skins, to stay calm in all circumstances and above all to take pleasure from gradually learning this beautiful profession that owes as much to Gutenberg as to the latest technologies.

To all of you reading this – in other words, those of you I haven't lost along the way because I couldn't retain everyone's attention on what can be tricky subjects – a big thank you!

INDEX

INDEX

ACKNOWLEDGEMENTS

All the experience I've accumulated over the course of my professional life would not have been enough to create this book. I have benefited from the valuable contributions of a number of accomplices:

Gilles Tarral, manufacturer and educationalist, places human relationships and productive dialogue at the very centre of his professional practice. He is the left brain of this book, the inspiration for the philosophy behind it and the creator of the keywords that have guided me in its writing.

If great perception skills and decision-making reside in the brain's right hemisphere, it is Caroline Moutier who has structured this book with her artistic direction and her masterful page layout expertise.

Throughout the writing of this book, I have relied on the unshakeable support of Antonio Maffeis, my long-standing accomplice, for whom inks, paper, and the machines and alchemy of printing have no secrets; and François Fert, the most gifted and knowledgeable of colour experts, who for countless years has translated my words into impeccable and reproducible images.

I would also like to thank the following people for their technical expertise: Christophe Roux, Apex Graphic and EtudeDK, as well as Céline Antoine, Thomas Drelon, Mara Mariano, Nicolas Perrier and Amélie Revil. Huge thanks to Barbara Gabrielli and Catia Celani for their unfailing vigilance, as well as all the team at D'Auria Printing.

The beautiful children's books published by Béatrice Decroix have enabled me to illustrate many of my ideas with images by Florence Guiraud, Frédéric Marais and Carine Deasay. A huge thank you to Catherine Noury, Anne-Lise Broyer, Clément Borderie and Nathalie Junod-Ponsard for their photos.

My editors, Céline Remechido and Christelle Doyelle, were the instigators and the driving force behind this book. I would like to thank them in particular for their commitment.

FOR THE ENGLISH EDITION

The publisher and translator would like to thank Alistair Morgan and the team at Bell & Bain Ltd printing company in Glasgow for their informative tour; Matt Dagwell, Hachette UK Paper Manager, for sharing his knowledge on paper; and technical readers Felicity Awdry, Davina Cheung, Sian Smith and Simon Walsh for bringing their invaluable expertise on terminology and practice. Thanks also to Marianne Lassandro for her role in bringing the English edition into being. And lastly, to Claire Keep at Quercus for skilfully steering the book through the production process.

ABOUT THE AUTHOR

Margherita Mariano holds a master's degree in French Literature from the University of Naples and has lived in France since the 1980s. She has worked in the print sector for over thirty-five years. She began learning her trade with the Mondadori Group, at a huge printing press in Verona. She subsequently worked for Arbook (a design studio specializing in beautiful illustrated books) and for EPA Editions, before starting her own company, Colourscan France, a subsidiary of one of the world's largest repro companies based in Singapore. Alongside this, she worked with printers and was commissioned by Flammarion to undertake her first full production supervision as a freelancer. In 1998, she created Ex Fabrica to continue developing this role. Since then, she has worked on one-off and multi-year assignments for small publishing houses, institutions and large companies as well as artists and authors who need support to self-publish. Margherita Mariano regularly gives training sessions on production as part of publishing courses.

Working with both prepress and printing, she has witnessed the technical evolutions in both fields through the eyes of an independent practitioner. She has always played an active role in the industry, thus validating her own working practices.

She continues to supervise technical and commercial relationships between her industrial partners in the print sector.

CREDITS

All computer graphics and illustrations are by Caroline Moutier.

All photographs are by Margherita Mariano except:

13: Quercus; 29: all rights reserved; 43: Shutterstock/Menno van der Haven; 47: Anne-Lise Broyer; 55: iStock; 56 left: all rights reserved; 56 centre and right: Keur of Champions; 59: iStock; 66: Catherine Noury; 70: Bibliothèque nationale de France; 71: Unsplash/billow926; 74: Catherine Noury; 75 top: Reproduced with permission of PEFC international; 75 bottom: FSC®; 87 top right: Catherine Noury; 91 bottom: Catherine Noury; 92: all rights reserved; 94: Shutterstock/Eagles Eyes X; 95: Caroline Moutier; 101: Caroline Moutier; 104: Catherine Noury; 107 left: Catherine Noury; 108 top: Shutterstock/Vagengeim; 108 centre: Shutterstock/De geppe; 108 bottom: Shutterstock/Andrey_Popov; 109: Epson; 114 right: Catherine Noury; 127: Quercus; 138 bottom: all rights reserved; 146 and 147: Unsplash/zacke-feller; 170: Catherine Noury; 171: Unsplash/Mika Baumeister; 172: Catherine Noury; 175: Catherine Noury; 184: all rights reserved; 197 bottom: Catherine Noury; 208 top left: Catherine Noury; 213: Catherine Noury; 217: Nina Poulsen; 218 top: Nina Poulsen; 219 bottom: Catherine Noury; 220: Catherine Noury; 221: Catherine Noury; 222 Right: Catherine Noury; 223: Nina Poulsen; 224 centre-left: Catherine Noury; 224 right: Julie Auzillon; 228 right: Gilles Rambaud; 229 right: Wintje van Rooijen; 230 top and centre-right: Catherine Noury; 230 bottom right: Nina Poulsen; 231 top right: Catherine Noury; 232 right: Catherine Noury; 233: Catherine Noury; 234 top: Catherine Noury; 235: Catherine Noury; 238: Catherine Noury; 239 left: Catherine Noury; 241 top: Nina Poulsen; 243 left: HOST; 243 top and centre-right: Nina Poulsen; 244 left: Catherine Noury; 244 right: Nina Poulsen; 246 top: Catherine Noury; 246 bottom: Nina Poulsen; 247 right: Catherine Noury; 249: Philippe Brulin; 251 right: all rights reserved; 252: all rights reserved; 255: all rights reserved.